MY MEDITERRANEAN WAY

EASY AND DELICIOUS RECIPES

LORENA VALLS

Table of Contents

Chicken Fiesta Salad

Preparation Time : 20 minutes

Cooking Time : 20 minutes

Servings : 4

Difficulty Level : Easy

Ingredients:

- 2 halves of chicken fillet without skin or bones
- 1 packet of herbs for fajitas, divided
- 1 tablespoon vegetable oil
- 1 can black beans, rinsed and drained
- 1 box of Mexican-style corn
- 1/2 cup of salsa
- 1 packet of green salad
- 1 onion, minced
- 1 tomato, quartered

Directions:

Rub the chicken evenly with 1/2 of the herbs for fajitas. Cook the oil in a frying pan over medium heat and cook the chicken for 8 minutes on the side by side or until the juice is clear; put aside. Combine beans, corn, salsa, and other 1/2 fajita spices in a large pan. Heat over medium heat until lukewarm. Prepare the salad by mixing green vegetables, onion, and tomato. Cover the chicken salad and dress the beans and corn mixture.

Nutrition (for 100g): 311 calories 6.4g fat 42.2g carbohydrates 23g protein 853mg sodium

Corn & Black Bean Salad

Preparation Time : 10 minutes

Cooking Time : 0 minutes

Servings : 4

Difficulty Level : Easy

Ingredients:

- 2 tablespoons vegetable oil
- 1/4 cup balsamic vinegar
- 1/2 teaspoon of salt
- 1/2 teaspoon of white sugar
- 1/2 teaspoon ground cumin
- 1/2 teaspoon ground black pepper
- 1/2 teaspoon chili powder
- 3 tablespoons chopped fresh coriander
- 1 can black beans (15 oz)
- 1 can of sweetened corn (8.75 oz) drained

Directions:

Combine balsamic vinegar, oil, salt, sugar, black pepper, cumin and chili powder in a small bowl. Combine black corn and beans in a medium bowl. Mix with vinegar and oil vinaigrette and garnish with coriander. Cover and refrigerate overnight.

Nutrition (for 100g): 214 calories 8.4 g fat 28.6g carbohydrates 7.5g protein 415mg sodium

Awesome Pasta Salad

Preparation Time : 30 minutes

Cooking Time : 10 minutes

Servings : 16

Difficulty Level : Average

Ingredients:

- 1 (16-oz) fusilli pasta package
- 3 cups of cherry tomatoes
- 1/2 pound of provolone, diced
- 1/2 pound of sausage, diced
- 1/4 pound of pepperoni, cut in half
- 1 large green pepper
- 1 can of black olives, drained
- 1 jar of chilis, drained
- 1 bottle (8 oz) Italian vinaigrette

Directions:

Boil a lightly salted water in a pot. Stir in the pasta and cook for about 8 to 10 minutes or until al dente. Drain and rinse with cold water.

Combine pasta with tomatoes, cheese, salami, pepperoni, green pepper, olives, and peppers in a large bowl. Pour the vinaigrette and mix well.

Nutrition (for 100g): 310 calories 17.7g fat 25.9g carbohydrates 12.9g protein 746mg sodium

Tuna Salad

Preparation Time : 20 minutes

Cooking Time : 0 minutes

Servings : 4

Difficulty Level : Easy

Ingredients:

- 1 (19 ounce) can of garbanzo beans
- 2 tablespoons mayonnaise
- 2 teaspoons of spicy brown mustard
- 1 tablespoon sweet pickle
- Salt and pepper to taste
- 2 chopped green onions

Directions:

Combine green beans, mayonnaise, mustard, sauce, chopped green onions, salt and pepper in a medium bowl. Mix well.

Nutrition (for 100g): 220 calories 7.2g fat 32.7g carbohydrates 7g protein 478mg sodium

Southern Potato Salad

Preparation Time : 15 minutes

Cooking Time : 15 minutes

Servings : 4

Difficulty Level : Average

Ingredients:

- 4 potatoes
- 4 eggs
- 1/2 stalk of celery, finely chopped
- 1/4 cup sweet taste
- 1 clove of garlic minced
- 2 tablespoons mustard
- 1/2 cup mayonnaise
- salt and pepper to taste

Directions:

Boil water in a pot then situate the potatoes and cook until soft but still firm, about 15 minutes; drain and chop. Transfer the eggs in a pan and cover with cold water.

Boil the water; cover, remove from heat, and let the eggs soak in hot water for 10 minutes. Remove then shell and chop.

Combine potatoes, eggs, celery, sweet sauce, garlic, mustard, mayonnaise, salt, and pepper in a large bowl. Mix and serve hot.

Nutrition (for 100g): 460 calories 27.4g fat 44.6g carbohydrates 11.3g protein 214mg sodium

Seven-Layer Salad

Preparation Time : 15 minutes

Cooking Time : 5 minutes

Servings : 10

Difficulty Level : Average

Ingredients:

- 1-pound bacon
- 1 head iceberg lettuce
- 1 red onion, minced
- 1 pack of 10 frozen peas, thawed
- 10 oz grated cheddar cheese
- 1 cup chopped cauliflower
- 1 1/4 cup mayonnaise
- 2 tablespoons white sugar
- 2/3 cup grated Parmesan cheese

Directions:

Put the bacon in a huge, shallow frying pan. Bake over medium heat until smooth. Crumble and set aside. Situate the chopped lettuce in a large bowl and cover with a layer of an onion, peas, grated cheese, cauliflower, and bacon.

Prepare the vinaigrette by mixing the mayonnaise, sugar, and parmesan cheese. Pour over the salad and cool to cool.

Nutrition (for 100g): 387 calories 32.7g fat 9.9g carbohydrates 14.5g protein 609mg sodium

Kale, Quinoa & Avocado Salad with Lemon Dijon Vinaigrette

Preparation Time : 5 minutes

Cooking Time : 25 minutes

Servings : 4

Difficulty Level : Difficult

Ingredients:

- 2/3 cup of quinoa
- 1 1/3 cup of water
- 1 bunch of kale, torn into bite-sized pieces
- 1/2 avocado - peeled, diced and pitted
- 1/2 cup chopped cucumber
- 1/3 cup chopped red pepper
- 2 tablespoons chopped red onion
- 1 tablespoon of feta crumbled

Directions:

Boil the quinoa and 1 1/3 cup of water in a pan. Adjust heat and simmer until quinoa is tender and water is absorbed for about 15 to 20 minutes. Set aside to cool.

Place the cabbage in a steam basket over more than an inch of boiling water in a pan. Seal the pan with a lid and steam until hot, about 45 seconds; transfer to a large plate. Garnish with cabbage, quinoa, avocado, cucumber, pepper, red onion, and feta cheese.

Combine olive oil, lemon juice, Dijon mustard, sea salt, and black pepper in a bowl until the oil is emulsified in the dressing; pour over the salad.

Nutrition (for 100g): 342 calories 20.3g fat 35.4g carbohydrates 8.9g protein 705mg sodium

Chicken Salad

Preparation Time : 20 minutes

Cooking Time : 0 minutes

Servings : 9

Difficulty Level : Easy

Ingredients:

- 1/2 cup mayonnaise
- 1/2 teaspoon of salt
- 3/4 teaspoon of poultry herbs
- 1 tablespoon lemon juice
- 3 cups cooked chicken breast, diced
- 1/4 teaspoon ground black pepper
- 1/4 teaspoon garlic powder
- 1/4 teaspoon onion powder
- 1/2 cup finely chopped celery
- 1 (8 oz) box of water chestnuts, drained and chopped
- 1/2 cup chopped green onions
- 1 1/2 cups green grapes cut in half
- 1 1/2 cups diced Swiss cheese

Directions:

Combine mayonnaise, salt, chicken spices, onion powder, garlic powder, pepper, and lemon juice in a medium bowl. Combine chicken, celery, green onions, water chestnuts, Swiss cheese, and raisins in a big bowl. Stir in the mayonnaise mixture and coat. Cool until ready to serve.

Nutrition (for 100g): 293 calories 19.5g fat 10.3g carbohydrates 19.4g protein 454mg sodium

Cobb Salad

Preparation Time : 5 minutes

Cooking Time : 15 minutes

Servings : 6

Difficulty Level : Difficult

Ingredients:

- 6 slices of bacon
- 3 eggs
- 1 cup Iceberg lettuce, grated
- 3 cups cooked minced chicken meat
- 2 tomatoes, seeded and minced
- 3/4 cup of blue cheese, crumbled
- 1 avocado - peeled, pitted and diced
- 3 green onions, minced
- 1 bottle (8 oz.) Ranch Vinaigrette

Directions:

Situate the eggs in a pan and soak them completely with cold water. Boil the water. Cover and remove from heat and let the eggs rest in hot water for 10 to 12 minutes. Remove from hot water, let cool, peel, and chop. Situate the bacon in a big, deep frying pan. Bake over medium heat until smooth. Set aside.

Divide the grated lettuce into separate plates. Spread chicken, eggs, tomatoes, blue cheese, bacon, avocado, and green onions in rows on lettuce. Sprinkle with your favorite vinaigrette and enjoy.

Nutrition (for 100g): 525 calories 39.9g fat 10.2g carbohydrates 31.7g protein 701mg sodium

Broccoli Salad

Preparation Time : 10 minutes

Cooking Time : 15 minutes

Servings : 6

Difficulty Level : Average

Ingredients:

- 10 slices of bacon
- 1 cup fresh broccoli
- ¼ cup red onion, minced
- ½ cup raisins
- 3 tablespoons white wine vinegar
- 2 tablespoons white sugar
- 1 cup mayonnaise
- 1 cup of sunflower seeds

Directions:

Cook the bacon in a deep-frying pan over medium heat. Drain, crumble, and set aside. Combine broccoli, onion, and raisins in a medium bowl. Mix vinegar, sugar, and mayonnaise in a small bowl. Pour over the broccoli mixture and mix. Cool for at least two hours.

Before serving, mix the salad with crumbled bacon and sunflower seeds.

Nutrition (for 100g): 559 calories 48.1g fat 31g carbohydrates 18g protein 584mg sodium

Strawberry Spinach Salad

Preparation Time : 10 minutes

Cooking Time : 0 minutes

Servings : 4

Difficulty Level : Easy

Ingredients:

- 2 tablespoons sesame seeds
- 1 tablespoon poppy seeds
- 1/2 cup white sugar
- 1/2 cup olive oil
- 1/4 cup distilled white vinegar
- 1/4 teaspoon paprika
- 1/4 teaspoon Worcestershire sauce
- 1 tablespoon minced onion
- 10 ounces fresh spinach
- 1-quart strawberries - cleaned, hulled and sliced
- 1/4 cup almonds, blanched and slivered

Directions:

In a medium bowl, whisk together the same seeds, poppy seeds, sugar, olive oil, vinegar, paprika, Worcestershire sauce, and onion. Cover, and chill for one hour.

In a large bowl, incorporate the spinach, strawberries, and almonds. Drizzle dressing over salad and toss. Refrigerate 10 to 15 minutes before serving.

Nutrition (for 100g): 491 calories 35.2g fat 42.9g carbohydrates 6g protein 691mg sodium

Pear Salad with Roquefort Cheese

Preparation Time : 20 minutes

Cooking Time : 10 minutes

Servings : 2

Difficulty Level : Average

Ingredients:

- 1 leaf lettuce, torn into bite-sized pieces
- 3 pears - peeled, cored and diced
- 5 ounces Roquefort, crumbled
- 1 avocado - peeled, seeded and diced
- 1/2 cup chopped green onions
- 1/4 cup white sugar
- 1/2 cup pecan nuts
- 1/3 cup olive oil
- 3 tablespoons red wine vinegar
- 1 1/2 teaspoon of white sugar
- 1 1/2 teaspoon of prepared mustard
- 1/2 teaspoon of salted black pepper
- 1 clove of garlic

Directions:

Stir in 1/4 cup of sugar with the pecans in a pan over medium heat. Continue to stir gently until the sugar caramelized with pecans. Cautiously transfer the nuts to wax paper. Let it chill and break into pieces.

Mix for vinaigrette oil, marinade, 1 1/2 teaspoon of sugar, mustard, chopped garlic, salt, and pepper.

In a deep bowl, combine lettuce, pears, blue cheese, avocado, and green onions. Put vinaigrette over salad, sprinkle with pecans and serve.

Nutrition (for 100g): 426 calories 31.6g fat 33.1g carbohydrates 8g protein 481mg sodium

Mexican Bean Salad

Preparation Time : 15 minutes

Cooking Time : 0 minutes

Servings : 6

Difficulty Level : Easy

Ingredients:

- 1 can black beans (15 oz), drained
- 1 can red beans (15 oz), drained
- 1 can white beans (15 oz), drained
- 1 green pepper, minced
- 1 red pepper, minced
- 1 pack of frozen corn kernels
- 1 red onion, minced
- 2 tablespoons fresh lime juice
- 1/2 cup olive oil
- 1/2 cup red wine vinegar
- 1 tablespoon lemon juice
- 1 tablespoon salt
- 2 tablespoons white sugar
- 1 clove of crushed garlic
- 1/4 cup chopped coriander
- 1/2 tablespoon ground cumin
- 1/2 tablespoon ground black pepper
- 1 dash of hot pepper sauce

- 1/2 teaspoon chili powder

Directions:

Combine beans, peppers, frozen corn, and red onion in a large bowl. Combine olive oil, lime juice, red wine vinegar, lemon juice, sugar, salt, garlic, coriander, cumin, and black pepper in a small bowl — season with hot sauce and chili powder.

Pour the vinaigrette with olive oil over the vegetables; mix well. Cool well and serve cold.

Nutrition (for 100g): 334 calories 14.8g fat 41.7g carbohydrates 11.2g protein 581mg sodium

Melon Salad

Preparation Time : 20 minutes

Cooking Time : 0 minutes

Servings : 6

Difficulty Level : Average

Ingredients:

- ¼ teaspoon sea salt
- ¼ teaspoon black pepper
- 1 tablespoon balsamic vinegar
- 1 cantaloupe, quartered & seeded
- 12 watermelon, small & seedless
- 2 cups mozzarella balls, fresh
- 1/3 cup basil, fresh & torn
- 2 tbsp. olive oil

Directions:

Scrape out balls of cantaloupe, and the place them in a colander over a serving bowl. Use your melon baller to cut the watermelon as well, and then put them in with your cantaloupe.

Allow your fruit to drain for ten minutes, and then refrigerate the juice for another recipe. It can even be added to smoothies. Wipe the bowl dry, and then place your fruit in it.

Add in your basil, oil, vinegar, mozzarella and tomatoes before seasoning with salt and pepper. Gently mix and serve immediately or chilled.

Nutrition (for 100g): 218 Calories 13g Fat 9g Carbohydrates 10g Protein 581mg Sodium

Orange Celery Salad

Preparation Time : 15 minutes

Cooking Time : 0 minutes

Servings : 6

Difficulty Level : Easy

Ingredients:

- 1 tablespoon lemon juice, fresh
- ¼ teaspoon sea salt, fine
- ¼ teaspoon black pepper
- 1 tablespoon olive brine
- 1 tablespoon olive oil
- ¼ cup red onion, sliced
- ½ cup green olives
- 2 oranges, peeled & sliced
- 3 celery stalks, sliced diagonally in ½ inch slices

Directions:

Put your oranges, olives, onion and celery in a shallow bowl. In a different bowl whisk your oil, olive brine and lemon juice, pour this over your salad. Season with salt and pepper before serving.

Nutrition (for 100g): 65 Calories 7g Fats 9g Carbohydrates 2g Protein 614mg Sodium

Roasted Broccoli Salad

Preparation Time : 20 minutes

Cooking Time : 10 minutes

Servings : 4

Difficulty Level : Difficult

Ingredients:

- 1 lb. broccoli, cut into florets & stem sliced
- 3 tablespoons olive oil, divided
- 1-pint cherry tomatoes
- 1 ½ teaspoons honey, raw & divided
- 3 cups cubed bread, whole grain
- 1 tablespoon balsamic vinegar
- ½ teaspoon black pepper
- ¼ teaspoon sea salt, fine
- grated parmesan for serving

Directions:

Prepare oven at 450 degrees, and then get out a rimmed baking sheet. Place it in the oven to heat up. Drizzle your broccoli with a tablespoon of oil, and toss to coat.

Remove the baking sheet form the oven, and spoon the broccoli on it. Leave oil it eh bottom of the bowl, add in your tomatoes, toss to coat, and then toss your tomatoes with a tablespoon of honey. Pour them on the same baking sheet as your broccoli.

Roast for fifteen minutes, and stir halfway through your cooking time. Add in your bread, and then roast for three more minutes. Whisk two tablespoons of oil, vinegar, and remaining honey. Season with salt and pepper. Pour this over your broccoli mix to serve.

Nutrition (for 100g): 226 Calories 12g Fat 26g Carbohydrates 7g Protein 581mg Sodium

Tomato Salad

Preparation Time : 20 minutes

Cooking Time : 0 minutes

Servings : 4

Difficulty Level : Easy

Ingredients:

- 1 cucumber, sliced
- ¼ cup sun dried tomatoes, chopped
- 1 lb. tomatoes, cubed
- ½ cup black olives
- 1 red onion, sliced
- 1 tablespoon balsamic vinegar
- ¼ cup parsley, fresh & chopped
- 2 tablespoons olive oil
- sea salt & black pepper to taste

Directions:

Get out a bowl and combine all of your vegetables together. To make your dressing mix all your seasoning, olive oil and vinegar. Toss with your salad and serve fresh.

Nutrition (for 100g): 126 Calories 9.2g Fat 11.5g Carbohydrates 2.1g Protein 681mg Sodium

Feta Beet Salad

Preparation Time : 15 minutes

Cooking Time : 0 minutes

Servings : 4

Difficulty Level : Easy

Ingredients:

- 6 red beets, cooked & peeled
- 3 ounces feta cheese, cubed
- 2 tablespoons olive oil
- 2 tablespoons balsamic vinegar

Directions:

Combine everything together, and then serve.

Nutrition (for 100g): 230 Calories 12g Fat 26.3g Carbohydrates 7.3g Protein 614mg Sodium

Cauliflower & Tomato Salad

Preparation Time : 15 minutes

Cooking Time : 0 minutes

Servings : 4

Difficulty Level : Easy

Ingredients:

- 1 head cauliflower, chopped
- 2 tablespoons parsley, fresh & chopped
- 2 cups cherry tomatoes, halved
- 2 tablespoons lemon juice, fresh
- 2 tablespoons pine nuts
- sea salt & black pepper to taste

Directions:

Mix your lemon juice, cherry tomatoes, cauliflower and parsley together, and then season. Top with pine nuts, and mix well before serving.

Nutrition (for 100g): 64 Calories 3.3g Fat 7.9g Carbohydrates 2.8g Protein 614mg Sodium

Pilaf with Cream Cheese

Preparation Time : 20 minutes

Cooking Time : 10 minutes

Servings : 6

Difficulty Level : Average

Ingredients:

- 2 cups yellow long grain rice, parboiled
- 1 cup onion
- 4 green onions
- 3 tablespoons butter
- 3 tablespoons vegetable broth
- 2 teaspoons cayenne pepper
- 1 teaspoon paprika
- ½ teaspoon cloves, minced
- 2 tablespoons mint leaves, fresh & chopped
- 1 bunch fresh mint leaves to garnish
- 1 tablespoons olive oil
- sea salt & black pepper to taste
- <u>Cheese Cream:</u>
- 3 tablespoons olive oil
- sea salt & black pepper to taste
- 9 ounces cream cheese

Directions:

Ready the oven at 360 degrees, and then pull out a pan. Heat your butter and olive oil together, and cook your onions and spring onions for two minutes.

Add in your salt, pepper, paprika, cloves, vegetable broth, rice and remaining seasoning. Sauté for three minutes. Wrap with foil, and bake for another half hour. Allow it to cool.

Mix in the cream cheese, cheese, olive oil, salt and pepper. Serve your pilaf garnished with fresh mint leaves.

Nutrition (for 100g): 364 Calories 30g Fat 20g Carbohydrates 5g Protein 511mg Sodium

Roasted Eggplant Salad

Preparation Time : 10 minutes

Cooking Time : 20 minutes

Servings : 6

Difficulty Level : Easy

Ingredients:

- 1 red onion, sliced
- 2 tablespoons parsley, fresh & chopped
- 1 teaspoon thyme
- 2 cups cherry tomatoes, halved
- sea salt & black pepper to taste
- 1 teaspoon oregano
- 3 tablespoons olive oil
- 1 teaspoon basil
- 3 eggplants, peeled & cubed

Directions:

Start by heating your oven to 350. Season your eggplant with basil, salt, pepper, oregano, thyme and olive oil. Situate it on a baking tray, and bake for a half hour. Toss with your remaining ingredients before serving.

Nutrition (for 100g): 148 Calories 7.7g Fat 20.5g Carbohydrates 3.5g Protein 660mg Sodium

Roasted Veggies

Preparation Time : 5 minutes

Cooking Time : 15 minutes

Servings : 12

Difficulty Level : Easy

Ingredients:

- 6 cloves garlic
- 6 tablespoons olive oil
- 1 fennel bulb, diced
- 1 zucchini, diced
- 2 red bell peppers, diced
- 6 potatoes, large & diced
- 2 teaspoons sea salt
- ½ cup balsamic vinegar
- ¼ cup rosemary, chopped & fresh
- 2 teaspoons vegetable bouillon powder

Directions:

Start by heating your oven to 400. Put your potatoes, fennel, zucchini, garlic and fennel on a baking dish, drizzling with olive oil. Sprinkle with salt, bouillon powder, and rosemary. Mix well, and then bake at 450 for thirty to forty minutes. Mix your vinegar into the vegetables before serving.

Nutrition (for 100g): 675 Calories 21g Fat 112g Carbohydrates 13g Protein 718mg Sodium

Pistachio Arugula Salad

Preparation Time : 20 minutes

Cooking Time : 0 minutes

Servings : 6

Difficulty Level : Easy

Ingredients:

- 6 cups kale, chopped
- ¼ cup olive oil
- 2 tablespoons lemon juice, fresh
- ½ teaspoon smoked paprika
- 2 cups arugula
- 1/3 cup pistachios, unsalted & shelled
- 6 tablespoons parmesan cheese, grated

Directions:

Get out a salad bowl and combine your oil, lemon, smoked paprika and kale. Gently massage the leaves for half a minute. Your kale should be coated well. Gently mix your arugula and pistachios when ready to serve.

Nutrition (for 100g): 150 Calories 12g Fat 8g Carbohydrates 5g Protein 637mg Sodium

Parmesan Barley Risotto

Preparation Time : 10 minutes

Cooking Time : 20 minutes

Servings : 6

Difficulty Level : Difficult

Ingredients:

- 1 cup yellow onion, chopped
- 1 tablespoon olive oil
- 4 cups vegetable broth, low sodium
- 2 cups pearl barley, uncooked
- ½ cup dry white wine
- 1 cup parmesan cheese, grated fine & divided
- sea salt & black pepper to taste
- fresh chives, chopped for serving
- lemon wedges for serving

Directions:

Add your broth into a saucepan and bring it to a simmer over medium-high heat. Get out a stock pot and put it over medium-high heat as well. Heat your oil before adding in your onion. Cook for eight minutes and stir occasionally. Add in your barley and cook for two minutes more. Stir in your barley, cooking until it's toasted.

Pour in the wine, cooking for a minute more. Most of the liquid should have evaporated before adding in a cup of warm broth. Cook and stir for two minutes. Your liquid should be absorbed. Add in the remaining broth by the cup, and cook until ach cup is absorbed. It should take about two minutes each time.

Pull out from the heat, add half a cup of cheese, and top with remaining cheese, chives, and lemon wedges.

Nutrition (for 100g): 345 Calories 7g Fat 56g Carbohydrates 14g Protein 912mg Sodium

Seafood & Avocado Salad

Preparation Time : 10 minutes

Cooking Time : 0 minutes

Servings : 4

Difficulty Level : Easy

Ingredients:

- 2 lbs. salmon, cooked & chopped
- 2 lbs. shrimp, cooked & chopped
- 1 cup avocado, chopped
- 1 cup mayonnaise
- 4 tablespoons lime juice, fresh
- 2 cloves garlic
- 1 cup sour cream
- sea salt & black pepper to taste
- ½ red onion, minced
- 1 cup cucumber, chopped

Directions:

Start by getting out a bowl and combine your garlic, salt, pepper, onion, mayonnaise, sour cream and lime juice,

Get out a different bowl and mix together your salmon, shrimp, cucumber, and avocado.

Add the mayonnaise mixture to your shrimp, and then allow it to sit for twenty minutes in the fridge before serving.

Nutrition (for 100g): 394 Calories 30g Fat 3g Carbohydrates 27g Protein 815mg Sodium

Mediterranean Shrimp Salad

Preparation Time : 40 minutes

Cooking Time : 0 minutes

Servings : 6

Difficulty Level : Easy

Ingredients:

- 1 ½ lbs. shrimp, cleaned & cooked
- 2 celery stalks, fresh
- 1 onion
- 2 green onions
- 4 eggs, boiled
- 3 potatoes, cooked
- 3 tablespoons mayonnaise
- sea salt & black pepper to taste

Directions:

Start by slicing your potatoes and chopping your celery. Slice your eggs, and season. Mix everything together. Put your shrimp over the eggs, and then serve with onion and green onions.

Nutrition (for 100g): 207 Calories 6g Fat 15g Carbohydrates 17g Protein 664mg Sodium

Chickpea Pasta Salad

Preparation Time : 10 minutes

Cooking Time : 15 minutes

Servings : 6

Difficulty Level : Average

Ingredients:

- 2 tablespoons olive oil
- 16 ounces rotelle pasta
- ½ cup cured olives, chopped
- 2 tablespoons oregano, fresh & minced
- 2 tablespoons parsley, fresh & chopped
- 1 bunch green onions, chopped
- ¼ cup red wine vinegar
- 15 ounces canned garbanzo beans, drained & rinsed
- ½ cup parmesan cheese, grated
- sea salt & black pepper to taste

Directions:

Boil water and put the pasta al dente and follow per package instructions. Drain it and rinse it using cold water.

Get out a skillet and heat your olive oil over medium heat. Add in your scallions, chickpeas, parsley, oregano and olives. Decrease the heat, and sauté for twenty minutes more. Allow this mixture to cool.

Toss your chickpea mixture with your pasta and add in your grated cheese, salt, pepper and vinegar. Let it chill for four hours or overnight before serving.

Nutrition (for 100g): 424 Calories 10g Fat 69g Carbohydrates 16g Protein 714mg Sodium

Mediterranean Stir Fry

Preparation Time : 10 minutes

Cooking Time : 30 minutes

Servings : 4

Difficulty Level : Average

Ingredients:

- 2 zucchinis
- 1 onion
- ¼ teaspoon sea salt
- 2 cloves garlic
- 3 teaspoons olive oil, divided
- 1 lb. chicken breasts, boneless
- 1 cup quick cooking barley
- 2 cups water
- ¼ teaspoon black pepper
- 1 teaspoon oregano
- ¼ teaspoon red pepper flakes
- ½ teaspoon basil
- 2 plum tomatoes
- ½ cup Greek olives, pitted
- 1 tablespoons parsley, fresh

Directions:

Start by removing the skin from your chicken, and then chop it into smaller pieces. Chop the garlic and parsley, and then chop your olives, zucchini, tomatoes and onions. Get out a saucepan and bring your water to a boil. Mix in your barley, letting it simmer for eight to ten minutes.

Turn off heat. Let it rest for five minutes. Get out a skillet and add in two teaspoons of olive oil. Stir fry your chicken once it's hot, and then remove it from heat. Cook the onion in your remaining oil. Mix in your remaining ingredients, and cook for an additional three to five minutes. Serve warm.

Nutrition (for 100g): 337 Calories 8.6g Fat 32.3g Carbohydrates 31.7g Protein 517mg Sodium

Balsamic Cucumber Salad

Preparation Time : 15 minutes

Cooking Time : 0 minutes

Servings : 4

Difficulty Level : Easy

Ingredients:

- 2/3 large English cucumber, halved and sliced
- 2/3 medium red onion, halved and thinly sliced
- 5 1/2 tablespoons balsamic vinaigrette
- 1 1/3 cups grape tomatoes, halved
- 1/2 cup crumbled reduced-fat feta cheese

Directions:

In a big bowl, mix cucumber, tomatoes and onion. Add vinaigrette; toss to coating. Refrigerate, covered, till serving. Just prior to serving, stir in cheese. Serve with a slotted teaspoon.

Nutrition (for 100g): 250 calories 12g fats 15g carbohydrates 34g protein 633mg Sodium

Beef Kefta Patties with Cucumber Salad

Preparation Time : 10 minutes

Cooking Time : 15 minutes

Servings : 2

Difficulty Level : Difficult

Ingredients:

- cooking spray
- 1/2-pound ground sirloin
- 2 tablespoons plus 2 tablespoons chopped fresh flat-leaf parsley, divided
- 1 1/2 teaspoons chopped peeled fresh ginger
- 1 teaspoon ground coriander
- 2 tablespoons chopped fresh cilantro
- 1/4 teaspoon salt
- 1/2 teaspoon ground cumin
- 1/4 teaspoon ground cinnamon
- 1 cup thinly sliced English cucumbers
- 1 tablespoon rice vinegar
- 1/4 cup plain fat-free Greek yogurt
- 1 1/2 teaspoons fresh lemon juice
- 1/4 teaspoon freshly ground black pepper
- 1 (6-inch) pitas, quartered

Directions:

Warmth a grill skillet over medium-high warmth. Coat pan with cooking spray. Combine beef, 1/4 glass parsley, cilantro, and next 5 elements in a medium bowl. Divide combination into 4 the same portions, shaping each into a 1/2-inch-thick patty. Add patties to pan; cook both sides until desired degree of doneness.

Mix cucumber and vinegar in a medium bowl; throw well. Combine fat-free yogurt, remaining 2 tablespoons parsley, juice, and pepper in a little bowl; stir with a whisk. Set up 1 patty and 1/2 cup cucumber mixture on each of 4 china. Top each offering with about 2 tablespoons yogurt spices. Serve each with 2 pita wedges.

Nutrition (for 100g): 116 calories 5g fats 11g carbohydrates 28g protein 642mg sodium

Chicken and Cucumber Salad with Parsley Pesto

Preparation Time : 15 minutes

Cooking Time : 5 minutes

Servings : 8

Difficulty Level : Easy

Ingredients:

- 2 2/3 cups packed fresh flat-leaf parsley leaves
- 1 1/3 cups fresh baby spinach
- 1 1/2 tablespoons toasted pine nuts
- 1 1/2 tablespoons grated Parmesan cheese
- 2 1/2 tablespoons fresh lemon juice
- 1 1/3 teaspoons kosher salt
- 1/3 teaspoon black pepper
- 1 1/3 medium garlic cloves, smashed
- 2/3 cup extra-virgin olive oil
- 5 1/3 cups shredded rotisserie chicken (from 1 chicken)
- 2 2/3 cups cooked shelled edamame
- 1 1/2 cans 1 (15-oz.) unsalted chickpeas, drained and rinsed
- 1 1/3 cups chopped English cucumbers
- 5 1/3 cups loosely packed arugula

Directions:

Combine parsley, spinach, lemon juice, pine nuts, cheese, garlic, salt, and pepper in food processor; process about 1 minute. With processor running, add oil; process until smooth, about 1 minute.

Stir together chicken, edamame, chickpeas, and cucumber in a large bowl. Add pesto; toss to combine.

Place 2/3 cup arugula in each of 6 bowls; top each with 1 cup chicken salad mixture. Serve immediately.

Nutrition (for 100g): 116 calories 12g fats 3g carbohydrates 9g protein 663mg sodium

Easy Arugula Salad

Preparation Time : 15 minutes

Cooking Time : 0 minutes

Servings : 6

Difficulty Level : Easy

Ingredients:

- 6 cups young arugula leaves, rinsed and dried
- 1 1/2 cups cherry tomatoes, halved
- 6 tablespoons pine nuts
- 3 tablespoons grapeseed oil or olive oil
- 1 1/2 tablespoons rice vinegar
- 3/8 teaspoon freshly ground black pepper to taste
- 6 tablespoons grated Parmesan cheese
- 3/4 teaspoon salt to taste
- 1 1/2 large avocados - peeled, pitted and sliced

Directions:

In a sizable plastic dish with a cover, incorporate arugula, cherry tomatoes, pine nut products, oil, vinegar, and Parmesan cheese. Period with salt and pepper to flavor. Cover, and wring to mix.

Separate salad onto china, and top with slices of avocado.

Nutrition (for 100g): 120 calories 12g fats 14g carbohydrates 25g protein 736mg sodium

Feta Garbanzo Bean Salad

Preparation Time : 10 minutes

Cooking Time : 0 minutes

Servings : 6

Difficulty Level : Easy

Ingredients:

- 1 1/2 cans (15 ounces) garbanzo beans
- 1 1/2 cans (2-1/4 ounces) sliced ripe olives, drained
- 1 1/2 medium tomatoes
- 6 tablespoons thinly sliced red onions
- 2 1/4 cups 1-1/2 coarsely chopped English cucumbers
- 6 tablespoons chopped fresh parsley
- 4 1/2 tablespoons olive oil
- 3/8 teaspoon salt
- 1 1/2 tablespoons lemon juice
- 3/16 teaspoon pepper
- 7 1/2 cups mixed salad greens
- 3/4 cup crumbled feta cheese

Directions:

Transfer all ingredients in a big bowl; toss to combine. Add parmesan cheese.

Nutrition (for 100g): 140 calories 16g fats 10g carbohydrates 24g protein 817mg sodium

Greek Brown and Wild Rice Bowls

Preparation Time : 15 minutes

Cooking Time : 5 minutes

Servings : 4

Difficulty Level : Easy

Ingredients:

- 2 packages (8-1/2 ounces) ready-to-serve whole grain brown and wild rice medley
- 1 medium ripe avocado, peeled and sliced
- 1 1/2 cups cherry tomatoes, halved
- 1/2 cup Greek vinaigrette, divided
- 1/2 cup crumbled feta cheese
- 1/2 cup pitted Greek olives, sliced
- minced fresh parsley, optional

Directions:

Inside a microwave-safe dish, mix the grain mix and 2 tablespoons vinaigrette. Cover and cook on high until warmed through, about 2 minutes. Divide between 2 bowls. Best with avocado, tomato vegetables, cheese, olives, leftover dressing and, if desired, parsley.

Nutrition (for 100g): 116 calories 10g fats 9g carbohydrates 26g protein 607mg sodium

Greek Dinner Salad

Preparation Time : 10 minutes

Cooking Time : 0 minutes

Servings : 4

Difficulty Level : Easy

Ingredients:

- 2 1/2 tablespoons coarsely chopped fresh parsley
- 2 tablespoons coarsely chopped fresh dill
- 2 teaspoons fresh lemon juice
- 2/3 teaspoon dried oregano
- 2 teaspoons extra virgin olive oil
- 4 cups shredded Romaine lettuce
- 2/3 cup thinly sliced red onions
- 1/2 cup crumbled feta cheese
- 2 cups diced tomatoes
- 2 teaspoons capers
- 2/3 cucumber, peeled, quartered lengthwise, and thinly sliced
- 2/3 (19-ounce) can chickpeas, drained and rinsed
- 4 (6-inch) whole wheat pitas, each cut into 8 wedges

Directions:

Combine the first 5 substances in a sizable dish; stir with a whisk. Add a member of the lettuce family and the next 6 ingredients (lettuce through chickpeas); throw well. Serve with pita wedges.

Nutrition (for 100g): 103 calories 12g fats 8g carbohydrates 36g protein 813mg sodium

Halibut with Lemon-Fennel Salad

Preparation Time : 15 minutes

Cooking Time : 5 minutes

Servings : 2

Difficulty Level : Average

Ingredients:

- 1/2 teaspoon ground coriander
- 1/4 teaspoon salt
- 1/8 teaspoon freshly ground black pepper
- 2 1/2 teaspoons extra-virgin olive oils, divided
- 1/4 teaspoon ground cumin
- 1 garlic clove, minced
- 2 (6-ounce) halibut fillets
- 1 cup fennel bulb
- 2 tablespoons thinly vertically sliced red onions
- 1 tablespoon fresh lemon juice
- 1 1/2 teaspoons chopped flat-leaf parsley
- 1/2 teaspoon fresh thyme leaves

Directions:

Combine the first 4 substances in a little dish. Combine 1/2 tsp spice mixture, 2 teaspoons oil, and garlic in a little bowl; rub garlic clove mixture evenly over fish. Heat 1 teaspoon oil in a sizable nonstick frying pan over medium-high high temperature. Add fish to pan; cook 5 minutes on each side or until the desired level of doneness.

Combine remaining 3/4 teaspoon spice mix, remaining 2 tsp oil, fennel light bulb, and remaining substances in a medium bowl, tossing well to coat. Provide salad with seafood.

Nutrition (for 100g): 110 calories 9g fats 11g carbohydrates 29g protein 558mg sodium

Herbed Greek Chicken Salad

Preparation Time : 10 minutes

Cooking Time : 10 minutes

Servings : 2

Difficulty Level : Average

Ingredients:

- 1/2 teaspoon dried oregano
- 1/4 teaspoon garlic powder
- 3/8 teaspoon black pepper, divided
- cooking spray
- 1/2-pound skinless, boneless chicken breasts, cut into 1-inch cubes
- 1/4 teaspoon salt, divided
- 1/2 cup plain fat-free yogurt
- 1 teaspoon tahini (sesame-seed paste)
- 2 1/2 tsps. fresh lemon juice
- 1/2 teaspoon bottled minced garlic
- 4 cups chopped Romaine lettuce
- 1/2 cup peeled chopped English cucumbers
- 1/2 cup grape tomatoes, halved
- 3 pitted kalamata olives, halved
- 2 tablespoons (1 ounce) crumbled feta cheese

Directions:

Combine oregano, garlic natural powder, 1/2 teaspoon pepper, and 1/4 tsp salt in a bowl. Heat a nonstick skillet over medium-high heat. Coating pan with cooking food spray. Add poultry and spice combination; sauté until poultry is done. Drizzle with 1 teaspoon juice; stir. Remove from pan.

Combine remaining 2 teaspoons juice, leftover 1/4 teaspoon sodium, remaining 1/4 tsp pepper, yogurt, tahini, and garlic in a little bowl; mix well. Combine member of the lettuce family, cucumber, tomatoes, and olives. Put 2 1/2 cups of lettuce mixture on each of 4 plates. Top each serving with 1/2 cup chicken combination and 1 teaspoon cheese. Drizzle each serving with 3 tablespoons yogurt combination

Nutrition (for 100g): 116 calories 11g fats 15g carbohydrates 28g protein 634mg sodium

Greek Couscous Salad

Preparation Time : 10 minutes

Cooking Time : 15 minutes

Servings : 10

Difficulty Level : Easy

Ingredients:

- 1 can (14-1/2 ounces) reduced-sodium chicken broth
- 1 1/2 cups 1-3/4 uncooked whole wheat couscous (about 11 ounces)
- Dressing:
- 6 1/2 tablespoons olive oil
- 1 1/4 teaspoons 1-1/2 grated lemon zest
- 3 1/2 tablespoons lemon juice
- 13/16 teaspoon adobo seasonings
- 3/16 teaspoon salt
- Salad:
- 1 2/3 cups grape tomatoes, halved
- 5/6 English cucumber, halved lengthwise and sliced
- 3/4 cup coarsely chopped fresh parsley
- 1 can (6-1/2 ounces) sliced ripe olives, drained
- 6 1/2 tablespoons crumbled feta cheese
- 3 1/3 green onions, chopped

Directions:

In a sizable saucepan, bring broth to a boil. Stir in couscous. Remove from heat; let stand, covered, until broth is absorbed, about 5 minutes. Transfer to a sizable dish; cool completely.

Beat together dressing substances. Add cucumber, tomato vegetables, parsley, olives and green onions to couscous; stir in dressing. Gently mix in cheese. Provide immediately or refrigerate and serve frosty.

Nutrition (for 100g): 114 calories 13g fats 18g carbohydrates 27g protein 811mg sodium

Denver Fried Omelet

Preparation Time : 10 minutes

Cooking Time : 30 minutes

Servings : 4

Difficulty Level : Average

Ingredients:

- 2 tablespoons butter
- 1/2 onion, minced meat
- 1/2 green pepper, minced
- 1 cup chopped cooked ham
- 8 eggs
- 1/4 cup of milk
- 1/2 cup grated cheddar cheese and ground black pepper to taste

Directions:

Preheat the oven to 200 degrees C (400 degrees F). Grease a round baking dish of 10 inches.

Melt the butter over medium heat; cook and stir onion and pepper until soft, about 5 minutes. Stir in the ham and keep cooking until everything is hot for 5 minutes.

Whip the eggs and milk in a large bowl. Stir in the mixture of cheddar cheese and ham; Season with salt and black pepper. Pour the mixture in a baking dish. Bake in the oven, about 25 minutes. Serve hot.

Nutrition (for 100g): 345 Calories 26.8g Fat 3.6g Carbohydrates 22.4g Protein 712 mg Sodium

Sausage Pan

Preparation Time : 25 minutes

Cooking Time : 60 minutes

Servings : 12

Difficulty Level : Average

Ingredients:

- 1-pound Sage Breakfast Sausage,
- 3 cups grated potatoes, drained and squeezed
- 1/4 cup melted butter,
- 12 oz soft grated Cheddar cheese
- 1/2 cup onion, grated
- 1 (16 oz) small cottage cheese container
- 6 giant eggs

Directions:

Set up the oven to 190 ° C. Grease a 9 x 13-inch square oven dish lightly.

Place the sausage in a big deep-frying pan. Bake over medium heat until smooth. Drain, crumble, and reserve.

Mix the grated potatoes and butter in the prepared baking dish. Cover the bottom and sides of the dish with the mixture. Combine in a bowl sausage, cheddar, onion, cottage cheese, and eggs. Pour over the potato mixture. Let it bake.

Allow cooling for 5 minutes before serving.

Nutrition (for 100g): 355 Calories 26.3g Fat 7.9g Carbohydrates 21.6g Protein 755mg Sodium.

Grilled Marinated Shrimp

Preparation Time : 30 minutes

Cooking Time : 60 minutes

Servings : 6

Difficulty Level : Easy

Ingredients:

- 1 cup olive oil,
- 1/4 cup chopped fresh parsley
- 1 lemon, juiced,
- 3 cloves of garlic, finely chopped
- 1 tablespoon tomato puree
- 2 teaspoons dried oregano,
- 1 teaspoon salt
- 2 tablespoons hot pepper sauce
- 1 teaspoon ground black pepper,
- 2 pounds of shrimp, peeled and stripped of tails

Directions:

Combine olive oil, parsley, lemon juice, hot sauce, garlic, tomato puree, oregano, salt, and black pepper in a bowl. Reserve a small amount to string later. Fill the large, resealable plastic bag with marinade and shrimp. Close and let it chill for 2 hours.

Preheat the grill on medium heat. Thread shrimp on skewers, poke once at the tail, and once at the head. Discard the marinade.

Lightly oil the grill. Cook the prawns for 5 minutes on each side or until they are opaque, often baste with the reserved marinade.

Nutrition (for 100g): 447 Calories 37.5g Fat 3.7g Carbohydrates 25.3g Protein 800mg Sodium

Sausage Egg Casserole

Preparation Time : 20 minutes

Cooking Time : 1 hour 10 minutes

Servings : 12

Difficulty Level : Average

Ingredients:

- 3/4-pound finely chopped pork sausage
- 1 tablespoon butter
- 4 green onions, minced meat
- 1/2 pound of fresh mushrooms
- 10 eggs, beaten
- 1 container (16 grams) low-fat cottage cheese
- 1 pound of Monterey Jack Cheese, grated
- 2 cans of a green pepper diced, drained
- 1 cup flour, 1 teaspoon baking powder
- 1/2 teaspoon salt
- 1/3 cup melted butter

Directions:

Put sausage in a deep-frying pan. Bake over medium heat until smooth. Drain and set aside. Melt the butter in a pan, cook and stir the green onions and mushrooms until they are soft.

Combine eggs, cottage cheese, Monterey Jack cheese, and peppers in a large bowl. Stir in sausages, green onions, and mushrooms. Cover and spend the night in the fridge.

Setup the oven to 175 ° C (350 ° F). Grease a 9 x 13-inch light baking dish.

Sift the flour, baking powder, and salt into a bowl. Stir in the melted butter. Incorporate flour mixture into the egg mixture. Pour into the prepared baking dish. Bake until lightly browned. Let stand for 10 minutes before serving.

Nutrition (for 100g): 408 Calories 28.7g Fat 12.4g Carbohydrates 25.2g Protein 1095mg Sodium

Baked Omelet Squares

Preparation Time : 15 minutes

Cooking Time : 30 minutes

Servings : 8

Difficulty Level : Easy

Ingredients:

- 1/4 cup butter
- 1 small onion, minced meat
- 1 1/2 cups grated cheddar cheese
- 1 can of sliced mushrooms
- 1 can slice black olives cooked ham (optional)
- sliced jalapeno peppers (optional)
- 12 eggs, scrambled eggs
- 1/2 cup of milk
- salt and pepper, to taste

Directions:

Prepare the oven to 205 ° C (400 ° F). Grease a 9 x 13-inch baking dish.

Cook the butter in a frying pan over medium heat and cook the onion until done.

Lay out the Cheddar cheese on the bottom of the prepared baking dish. Layer with mushrooms, olives, fried onion, ham, and jalapeno peppers. Stir the eggs in a bowl with milk, salt, and pepper. Pour the egg mixture over the ingredients, but do not mix.

Bake in the uncovered and preheated oven, until no more liquid flows in the middle and is light brown above. Allow to cool a little, then cut it into squares and serve.

Nutrition (for 100g): 344 Calories 27.3g Fat 7.2g Carbohydrates 17.9g Protein 1087mg Sodium

Hard-Boiled Egg

Preparation Time : 5 minutes

Cooking Time : 15 minutes

Servings : 8

Difficulty Level : Easy

Ingredients:

- 1 tablespoon of salt
- 1/4 cup distilled white vinegar
- 6 cups of water
- 8 eggs

Directions:

Place the salt, vinegar, and water in a large saucepan and bring to a boil over high heat. Stir in the eggs one by one, and be careful not to split them. Lower the heat and cook over low heat and cook for 14 minutes.

Pull out the eggs from the hot water and place them in a container filled with ice water or cold water. Cool completely, approximately 15 minutes.

Nutrition (for 100g): 72 Calories 5g Fat 0.4g Carbohydrates 6.3g Protein 947 mg Sodium

Mushrooms with a Soy Sauce Glaze

Preparation Time : 5 minutes

Cooking Time : 10 minutes

Servings : 2

Difficulty Level : Average

Ingredients:

- 2 tablespoons butter
- 1(8 ounces) package sliced white mushrooms
- 2 cloves garlic, minced
- 2 teaspoons soy sauce
- ground black pepper to taste

Directions:

Cook the butter in a frying pan over medium heat; stir in the mushrooms; cook and stir until the mushrooms are soft and released about 5 minutes. Stir in the garlic; keep cooking and stir for 1 minute. Pour the soy sauce; cook the mushrooms in the soy sauce until the liquid has evaporated, about 4 minutes.

Nutrition (for 100g): 135 Calories 11.9g Fat 5.4g Carbohydrates

Pepperoni Eggs

Preparation Time : 10 minutes

Cooking Time : 20 minutes

Servings : 2

Difficulty Level : Average

Ingredients:

- 1 cup of egg substitute
- 1 egg
- 3 green onions, minced meat
- 8 slices of pepperoni, diced
- 1/2 teaspoon of garlic powder
- 1 teaspoon melted butter
- 1/4 cup grated Romano cheese
- salt and ground black pepper to taste

Directions:

Combine the egg substitute, the egg, the green onions, the pepperoni slices, and the garlic powder in a bowl.

Cook the butter in a non-stick frying pan over low heat; Add the egg mixture, seal the pan and cook 10 to 15 minutes. Sprinkle Romano's eggs and season with salt and pepper.

Nutrition (for 100g): 266 Calories 16.2g Fat 3.7g Carbohydrates 25.3g Protein 586mg Sodium

Egg Cupcakes

Preparation Time : 15 minutes

Cooking Time : 20 minutes

Servings : 6

Difficulty Level : Average

Ingredients:

- 1 pack of bacon (12 ounces)
- 6 eggs
- 2 tablespoons of milk
- 1/4 teaspoon salt
- 1/4 teaspoon ground black pepper
- 1 c. Melted butter
- 1/4 teaspoon. Dried parsley
- 1/2 cup ham
- 1/4 cup mozzarella cheese
- 6 slices gouda

Directions:

Prepare the oven to 175 ° C (350 ° F). Cook bacon over medium heat, until it starts to brown. Dry the bacon slices with kitchen paper.

Situate the slices of bacon in the 6 cups of the non-stick muffin pan. Slice the remaining bacon and put it at the bottom of each cup.

Mix eggs, milk, butter, parsley, salt, and pepper. Add in the ham and mozzarella cheese.

Fill the cups with the egg mixture; garnish with Gouda cheese.

Bake in the preheated oven until Gouda cheese is melted and the eggs are tender about 15 minutes.

Nutrition (for 100g): 310 Calories 22.9g Fat 2.1g Carbohydrates 23.1g Protein 988mg Sodium.

Dinosaur Eggs

Preparation Time : 20 minutes

Cooking Time : 15 minutes

Servings : 4

Difficulty Level : Difficult

Ingredients:

- Mustard sauce:
- 1/4 cup coarse mustard
- 1/4 cup Greek yogurt
- 1 teaspoon garlic powder
- 1 pinch of cayenne pepper
- Eggs:
- 2 beaten eggs
- 2 cups of mashed potato flakes
- 4 boiled eggs, peeled
- 1 can (15 oz) HORMEL® Mary Kitchen® minced beef finely chopped can
- 2 liters of vegetable oil for frying

Directions:

Combine the old-fashioned mustard, Greek yogurt, garlic powder, and cayenne pepper in a small bowl until smooth.

Transfer the 2 beaten eggs in a shallow dish; place the potato flakes in a separate shallow dish.

Divide the minced meat into 4 Servings. Form salted beef around each egg until it is completely wrapped.

Soak the wrapped eggs in the beaten egg and brush with mashed potatoes until they are covered.

Fill the oil in a large saucepan and heat at 190 ° C (375 ° F).

Put 2 eggs in the hot oil and bake for 3 to 5 minutes until brown. Remove with a drop of spoon and place on a plate lined with kitchen paper. Repeat this with the remaining 2 eggs.

Cut lengthwise and serve with a mustard sauce.

Nutrition (for 100g): 784 Calories 63.2g Fat 34g Carbohydrates

Dill and Tomato Frittata

Preparation Time : 10 minutes

Cooking Time : 35 minutes

Servings : 6

Difficulty Level : Average

Ingredients:

- Pepper and salt to taste
- 1 teaspoon red pepper flakes
- 2 garlic cloves, minced
- ½ cup crumbled goat cheese – optional
- 2 tablespoon fresh chives, chopped
- 2 tablespoon fresh dill, chopped
- 4 tomatoes, diced
- 8 eggs, whisked
- 1 teaspoon coconut oil

Directions:

Grease a 9-inch round baking pan and preheat oven to 325oF.

In a large bowl, mix well all ingredients and pour into prepped pan.

Lay into the oven and bake until middle is cooked through around 30-35 minutes.

Remove from oven and garnish with more chives and dill.

Nutrition (for 100g): 149 Calories 10.28g Fat 9.93g Carbohydrates 13.26g Protein 523mg Sodium

Paleo Almond Banana Pancakes

Preparation Time : 10 minutes

Cooking Time : 10 minutes

Servings : 3

Difficulty Level : Average

Ingredients:

- ¼ cup almond flour
- ½ teaspoon ground cinnamon
- 3 eggs
- 1 banana, mashed
- 1 tablespoon almond butter
- 1 teaspoon vanilla extract
- 1 teaspoon olive oil
- Sliced banana to serve

Directions:

Whip eggs in a bowl until fluffy. In another bowl, mash the banana using a fork and add to the egg mixture. Add the vanilla, almond butter, cinnamon and almond flour. Mix into a smooth batter. Heat the olive oil in a skillet. Add one spoonful of the batter and fry them on both sides.

Keep doing these steps until you are done with all the batter.

Add some sliced banana on top before serving.

Nutrition (for 100g): 306 Calories 26g Fat 3.6g Carbohydrates 14.4g Protein 588mg Sodium

Zucchini with Egg

Preparation Time : 5 minutes

Cooking Time : 10 minutes

Servings : 2

Difficulty Level : Easy

Ingredients:

- 1 1/2 tablespoons olive oil
- 2 large zucchinis, cut into large chunks
- salt and ground black pepper to taste
- 2 large eggs
- 1 teaspoon water, or as desired

Directions:

Cook the oil in a frying pan over medium heat; sauté zucchini until soft, about 10 minutes. Season the zucchini well.

Lash the eggs using a fork in a bowl. Pour in water and beat until everything is well mixed. Pour the eggs over the zucchini; boil and stir until scrambled eggs and no more flowing, about 5 minutes. Season well the zucchini and eggs.

Nutrition (for 100g): 213 Calories 15.7g Fat 11.2g Carbohydrates 10.2g Protein 180mg Sodium

Cheesy Amish Breakfast Casserole

Preparation Time : 10 minutes

Cooking Time : 50 minutes

Servings : 12

Difficulty Level : Easy

Ingredients:

- 1-pound sliced bacon, diced,
- 1 sweet onion, minced meat
- 4 cups grated and frozen potatoes, thawed
- 9 lightly beaten eggs
- 2 cups of grated cheddar cheese
- 1 1/2 cup of cottage cheese
- 1 1/4 cups of grated Swiss cheese

Directions:

Preheat the oven to 175 ° C (350 ° F). Grease a 9 x 13-inch baking dish.

Warm up large frying pan over medium heat; cook and stir the bacon and onion until the bacon is evenly browned about 10 minutes. Drain. Stir in potatoes, eggs, cheddar cheese, cottage cheese, and Swiss cheese. Fill the mixture into a prepared baking dish.

Bake in the oven until the eggs are cooked and the cheese is melted 45 to 50 minutes. Set aside for 10 minutes before cutting and serving.

Nutrition (for 100g): 314 Calories 22.8g Fat 12.1g Carbohydrates 21.7g Protein 609mg Sodium

Salad with Roquefort Cheese

Preparation Time : 20 minutes

Cooking Time : 25 minutes

Servings : 6

Difficulty Level : Easy

Ingredients:

- 1 leaf lettuce, torn into bite-sized pieces
- 3 pears - peeled, without a core and cut into pieces
- 5 oz Roquefort cheese, crumbled
- 1/2 cup chopped green onions
- 1 avocado - peeled, seeded and diced
- 1/4 cup white sugar
- 1/2 cup pecan nuts
- 1 1/2 teaspoon white sugar
- 1/3 cup olive oil,
- 3 tablespoons red wine vinegar,
- 1 1/2 teaspoons prepared mustard,
- 1 clove of chopped garlic,
- 1/2 teaspoon ground fresh black pepper

Directions:

Incorporate 1/4 cup of sugar with the pecans in a frying pan over medium heat. Continue to stir gently until the sugar has melted with pecans. Carefully situate the nuts to wax paper. Set aside and break into pieces.

Combination for vinaigrette oil, vinegar, 1 1/2 teaspoon of sugar, mustard, chopped garlic, salt, and pepper.

In a large bowl, mix lettuce, pears, blue cheese, avocado, and green onions. Pour vinaigrette over salad, topped with pecans and serve.

Nutrition (for 100g): 426 Calories 31.6g Fat 33.1g Carbohydrates 8g Protein 654mg Sodium

Rice with Vermicelli

Preparation Time : 5 minutes

Cooking Time : 45 minutes

Servings : 6

Difficulty Level : Easy

Ingredients:

- 2 cups short-grain rice
- 3½ cups water, plus more for rinsing and soaking the rice
- ¼ cup olive oil
- 1 cup broken vermicelli pasta
- Salt

Directions:

Soak the rice under cold water until the water runs clean. Place the rice in a bowl, cover with water, and let soak for 10 minutes. Drain and set aside. Cook the olive oil in a medium pot over medium heat.

Stir in the vermicelli and cook for 2 to 3 minutes, stirring continuously, until golden.

Put the rice and cook for 1 minute, stirring, so the rice is well coated in the oil. Stir in the water and a pinch of salt and bring the liquid to a boil. Adjust heat and simmer for 20 minutes. Pull out from the heat and let rest for 10 minutes. Fluff with a fork and serve.

Nutrition (for 100g): 346 calories 9g total fat 60g carbohydrates 2g protein 0.9mg sodium

Fava Beans and Rice

Preparation Time : 10 minutes

Cooking Time : 35 minutes

Servings : 4

Difficulty Level : Easy

Ingredients:

- ¼ cup olive oil
- 4 cups fresh fava beans, shelled
- 4½ cups water, plus more for drizzling
- 2 cups basmati rice
- 1/8 teaspoon salt
- 1/8 teaspoon freshly ground black pepper
- 2 tablespoons pine nuts, toasted
- ½ cup chopped fresh garlic chives, or fresh onion chives

Directions:

Fill the sauce pan with olive oil and cook over medium heat. Add the fava beans and drizzle them with a bit of water to avoid burning or sticking. Cook for 10 minutes.

Gently stir in the rice. Add the water, salt, and pepper. Set up the heat and boil the mixture. Adjust the heat and let it simmer for 15 minutes.

Pull out from the heat and let it rest for 10 minutes before serving. Spoon onto a serving platter and sprinkle with the toasted pine nuts and chives.

Nutrition (for 100g): 587 calories 17g total fat 97g carbohydrates 2g protein 0.6mg sodium

Buttered Fava Beans

Preparation Time : 30 minutes

Cooking Time : 15 minutes

Servings : 4

Difficulty Level : Easy

Ingredients:

- ½ cup vegetable broth
- 4 pounds fava beans, shelled
- ¼ cup fresh tarragon, divided
- 1 teaspoon chopped fresh thyme
- ¼ teaspoon freshly ground black pepper
- 1/8 teaspoon salt
- 2 tablespoons butter
- 1 garlic clove, minced
- 2 tablespoons chopped fresh parsley

Directions:

Boil vegetable broth in a shallow pan over medium heat. Add the fava beans, 2 tablespoons of tarragon, the thyme, pepper, and salt. Cook until the broth is almost absorbed and the beans are tender.

Stir in the butter, garlic, and remaining 2 tablespoons of tarragon. Cook for 2 to 3 minutes. Sprinkle with the parsley and serve hot.

Nutrition (for 100g): 458 calories 9g fat 81g carbohydrates 37g protein 691mg sodium

Freekeh

Preparation Time : 10 minutes

Cooking Time : 40 minutes

Servings : 4

Difficulty Level : Easy

Ingredients:

- 4 tablespoons Ghee
- 1 onion, chopped
- 3½ cups vegetable broth
- 1 teaspoon ground allspice
- 2 cups freekeh
- 2 tablespoons pine nuts, toasted

Directions:

Melt ghee in a heavy-bottomed saucepan over medium heat. Stir in the onion and cook for about 5 minutes, stirring constantly, until the onion is golden. Pour in the vegetable broth, add the allspice, and bring to a boil. Stir in the freekeh and return the mixture to a boil. Adjust heat and simmer for 30 minutes, stir occasionally. Spoon the freekeh into a serving dish and top with the toasted pine nuts.

Nutrition (for 100g): 459 calories 18g fat 64g carbohydrates 10g protein 692mg sodium

Fried Rice Balls with Tomato Sauce

Preparation Time : 15 minutes

Cooking Time : 20 minutes

Servings : 8

Difficulty Level : Difficult

Ingredients:

- 1 cup bread crumbs
- 2 cups cooked risotto
- 2 large eggs, divided
- ¼ cup freshly grated Parmesan cheese
- 8 fresh baby mozzarella balls, or 1 (4-inch) log fresh mozzarella, cut into 8 pieces
- 2 tablespoons water
- 1 cup corn oil
- 1 cup Basic Tomato Basil Sauce, or store-bought

Directions:

Situate the bread crumbs into a small bowl and set aside. In a medium bowl, stir together the risotto, 1 egg, and the Parmesan cheese until well. Split the risotto mixture into 8 pieces. Situate them on a clean work surface and flatten each piece.

Place 1 mozzarella ball on each flattened rice disk. Close the rice around the mozzarella to form a ball. Repeat until you finish all the balls. In the same medium, now-empty bowl, whisk the remaining egg and the water. Dip each prepared risotto ball into the egg wash and roll it in the bread crumbs. Set aside.

Cook corn oil in a skillet over high heat. Gently lower the risotto balls into the hot oil and fry for 5 to 8 minutes until golden brown. Stir them, as needed, to ensure the entire surface is fried. Using a slotted spoon, put the fried balls to paper towels to drain.

Warm up the tomato sauce in a medium saucepan over medium heat for 5 minutes, stir occasionally, and serve the warm sauce alongside the rice balls.

Nutrition (for 100g): 255 calories 15g fat 16g carbohydrates 2g protein 669mg sodium

Spanish-Style Rice

Preparation Time : 10 minutes

Cooking Time : 35 minutes

Servings : 4

Difficulty Level : Average

Ingredients:

- ¼ cup olive oil
- 1 small onion, finely chopped
- 1 red bell pepper, seeded and diced
- 1½ cups white rice
- 1 teaspoon sweet paprika
- ½ teaspoon ground cumin
- ½ teaspoon ground coriander
- 1 garlic clove, minced
- 3 tablespoons tomato paste
- 3 cups vegetable broth
- 1/8 teaspoon salt

Directions:

Cook the olive oil in a large heavy-bottomed skillet over medium heat. Stir in the onion and red bell pepper. Cook for 5 minutes or until softened. Add the rice, paprika, cumin, and coriander and cook for 2 minutes, stirring often.

Add the garlic, tomato paste, vegetable broth, and salt. Stir it well and season, as needed. Allow the mixture to a boil. Lower heat and simmer for 20 minutes.

Set aside for 5 minutes before serving.

Nutrition (for 100g): 414 calories 14g fat 63g carbohydrates 2g protein 664mg sodium

Zucchini with Rice and Tzatziki

Preparation Time : 20 minutes

Cooking Time : 35 minutes

Servings : 4

Difficulty Level : Average

Ingredients:

- ¼ cup olive oil
- 1 onion, chopped
- 3 zucchinis, diced
- 1 cup vegetable broth
- ½ cup chopped fresh dill
- Salt
- Freshly ground black pepper
- 1 cup short-grain rice
- 2 tablespoons pine nuts
- 1 cup Tzatziki Sauce, Plain Yogurt, or store-bought

Directions:

Cook oil in a heavy-bottomed pot over medium heat. Stir in the onion, turn the heat to medium-low, and sauté for 5 minutes. Mix in the zucchini and cook for 2 minutes more.

Stir in the vegetable broth and dill and season with salt and pepper. Turn up heat to medium and bring the mixture to a boil.

Stir in the rice and place the mixture back to a boil. Set the heat to very low, cover the pot, and cook for 15 minutes. Pull out from the heat and set aside, for 10 minutes. Scoop the rice onto a serving platter, sprinkle with the pine nuts, and serve with tzatziki sauce.

Nutrition (for 100g): 414 calories 17g fat 57g carbohydrates 5g protein 591mg sodium

Cannellini Beans with Rosemary and Garlic Aioli

Preparation Time : 10 minutes

Cooking Time : 10 minutes

Servings : 4

Difficulty Level : Easy

Ingredients:

- 4 cups cooked cannellini beans
- 4 cups water
- ½ teaspoon salt
- 3 tablespoons olive oil
- 2 tablespoons chopped fresh rosemary
- ½ cup Garlic Aioli
- ¼ teaspoon freshly ground black pepper

Directions:

Mix the cannellini beans, water, and salt in a medium saucepan over medium heat. Bring to a boil. Cook for 5 minutes. Drain. Cook the olive oil in a skillet over medium heat.

Add the beans. Stir in the rosemary and aioli. Adjust heat to medium-low and cook, stirring, just to heat through. Season with pepper and serve.

Nutrition (for 100g): 545 calories 36g fat 42g carbohydrates 14g protein 608mg sodium

Jeweled Rice

Preparation Time : 15 minutes

Cooking Time : 30 minutes

Servings : 6

Difficulty Level : Difficult

Ingredients:

- ½ cup olive oil, divided
- 1 onion, finely chopped
- 1 garlic clove, minced
- ½ teaspoon chopped peeled fresh ginger
- 4½ cups water
- 1 teaspoon salt, divided, plus more as needed
- 1 teaspoon ground turmeric
- 2 cups basmati rice
- 1 cup fresh sweet peas
- 2 carrots, peeled and cut into ½-inch dice
- ½ cup dried cranberries
- Grated zest of 1 orange
- 1/8 teaspoon cayenne pepper
- ¼ cup slivered almonds, toasted

Directions:

Warm up ¼ cup of olive oil in a large pan. Place the onion and cook for 4 minutes. Sauté in the garlic and ginger.

Stir in the water, ¾ teaspoon of salt, and the turmeric. Bring the mixture to a boil. Put in the rice and return the mixture to a boil. Taste the broth and season with more salt, as needed. Select the heat to low, and cook for 15 minutes. Turn off the heat. Let the rice rest on the burner, covered, for 10 minutes. Meanwhile, in a medium sauté pan or skillet over medium-low heat, heat the remaining ¼ cup of olive oil. Stir in the peas and carrots. Cook for 5 minutes.

Stir in the cranberries and orange zest. Dust with the remaining salt and the cayenne. Cook for 1 to 2 minutes. Spoon the rice onto a serving platter. Top with the peas and carrots and sprinkle with the toasted almonds.

Nutrition (for 100g): 460 calories 19g fat 65g carbohydrates 4g protein 810mg sodium

Asparagus Risotto

Preparation Time : 15 minutes

Cooking Time : 30 minutes

Servings : 4

Difficulty Level : Difficult

Ingredients:

- 5 cups vegetable broth, divided
- 3 tablespoons unsalted butter, divided
- 1 tablespoon olive oil
- 1 small onion, chopped
- 1½ cups Arborio rice
- 1-pound fresh asparagus, ends trimmed, cut into 1-inch pieces, tips separated
- ¼ cup freshly grated Parmesan cheese

Directions:

Boil the vegetable broth over medium heat. Set the heat to low and simmer. Mix 2 tablespoons of butter with the olive oil. Stir in the onion and cook for 2 to 3 minutes.

Put the rice and stir with a wooden spoon while cooking for 1 minute until the grains are well covered with butter and oil.

Stir in ½ cup of warm broth. Cook and continue stirring until the broth is completely absorbed. Add the asparagus stalks and another ½ cup of broth. Cook and stir occasionally Continue adding the broth, ½ cup at a time, and cooking until it is completely absorbed upon adding the next ½ cup. Stir frequently to prevent sticking. Rice should be cooked but still firm.

Add the asparagus tips, the remaining 1 tablespoon of butter, and the Parmesan cheese. Stir vigorously to combine. Remove from the heat, top with additional Parmesan cheese, if desired, and serve immediately.

Nutrition (for 100g): 434 calories 14g fat 67g carbohydrates 6g protein 517mg sodium

Seafood Linguine

Preparation Time : 10 minutes

Cooking Time : 35 minutes

Servings : 2

Difficulty Level : Difficult

Ingredients:

- 2 Cloves Garlic, Chopped
- 4 Ounces Linguine, Whole Wheat
- 1 Tablespoon Olive Oil
- 14 Ounces Tomatoes, Canned & Diced
- 1/2 Tablespoon Shallot, Chopped
- 1/4 Cup White Wine
- Sea Salt & Black Pepper to Taste
- 6 Cherrystone Clams, Cleaned
- 4 Ounces Tilapia, Sliced into 1 Inch Strips
- 4 Ounces Dry Sea Scallops
- 1/8 Cup Parmesan Cheese, Grated
- 1/2 Teaspoon Marjoram, Chopped & Fresh

Directions:

Boil the water in pot, then cook pasta until tender which should take roughly eight minutes. Drain and then rinse your pasta.

Heat your oil using a large skillet over medium heat, and then once your oil is hot stir in your garlic and shallot. Cook for a minute, and stir often.

Increase the heat to medium-high before adding your salt, wine, pepper and tomatoes, bringing it to a simmer. Cook for one minute more.

Add your clams next, covering and cooking for another two minutes.

Stir in your marjoram, scallops and fish next. Continue cooking until the fish is cook all the way through and your clams have opened up this will take up to five minutes, and get rid of any clams that do not open.

Spoon the sauce and your clams over the pasta, sprinkling with parmesan and marjoram before serving. Serve warm.

Nutrition (for 100g): 329 calories 12g fats 10g carbohydrates 33g protein 836mg sodium

Ginger Shrimp & Tomato Relish

Preparation Time : 10 minutes

Cooking Time : 15 minutes

Servings : 2

Difficulty Level : Difficult

Ingredients:

- 1 1/2 Tablespoons Vegetable Oil
- 1 Clove Garlic, Minced
- 10 Shrimp, Extra Large, Peeled & Tails Left On
- 3/4 Tablespoons Finger, Grated & Peeled
- 1 Green Tomatoes, Halved
- 2 Plum Tomatoes, Halved
- 1 Tablespoon Lime Juice, Fresh
- 1/2 Teaspoon Sugar
- 1/2 Tablespoon Jalapeno with Seeds, Fresh & Minced
- 1/2 Tablespoon Basil, Fresh & Chopped
- 1/2 Tablespoons Cilantro, Chopped & Fresh
- 10 Skewers
- Sea Salt & Black Pepper to Taste

Directions:

Immerse your skewers in a pan of water for at least a half hour.

Stir your garlic and ginger together in a bowl, transferring half to a larger bowl and stirring it with two tablespoons of your oil. Add in the shrimp, and make sure they are well coated.

Cover and transfer it in the fridge for at least a half hour, and then allow it to refrigerate.

Heat your grill to high, and grease the grates lightly using oil. Get out a bowl and toss your plum and green tomatoes with the remaining tablespoon of oil, seasoning with salt and pepper.

Grill your tomatoes with the cut side up and the skins should be charred. The flesh of your tomato should be tender, which will take about four to six minutes for the plum tomato and about ten minutes for the green tomato.

Remove the skins once the tomatoes are cool enough to handle, and then discard the seeds. Chop the tomatoes flesh fine, adding it to the reserved ginger and garlic. Add in your sugar, jalapeno, lime juice and basil.

Season your shrimp using salt and pepper threading them onto the skewers, and then grill until they turn opaque, which is about two minutes on each side. Place the shrimp on a platter with your relish and enjoy.

Nutrition (for 100g): 391 calories 13g fats 11g carbohydrates 34g protein 693mg sodium

Shrimp & Pasta

Preparation Time : 10 minutes

Cooking Time : 10 minutes

Servings : 2

Difficulty Level : Average

Ingredients:

- 2 Cups Angel Hair Pasta, Cooked
- 1/2 lb. Medium Shrimp, Peeled
- 1 Clove Garlic, Minced
- 1 Cup Tomato, Chopped
- 1 Teaspoon Olive Oil
- 1/6 Cup Kalamata Olives, Pitted & Chopped
- 1/8 Cup Basil, Fresh & Sliced Thin
- 1 Tablespoon Capers, Drained
- 1/8 Cup Feta Cheese, Crumbled
- Dash Black Pepper

Directions:

Cook your pasta per package instructions, and then heat your olive oil in a skillet using medium-high heat. Cook your garlic for half a minute, and then add your shrimp. Sauté for a minute more.

Add your basil and tomato, and then reduce the heat to allow it to simmer for three minutes. Your tomato should be tender.

Stir in your olives and capers. Add a dash of black pepper, and combine your shrimp mix and pasta to serve. Top with cheese before serving warm.

Nutrition (for 100g): 357 calories 11g fats 9g carbohydrates 30g protein 871mg sodium

Poached Cod

Preparation Time : 10 minutes

Cooking Time : 25 minutes

Servings : 2

Difficulty Level : Average

Ingredients:

- 2 Cod Filets, 6 Ounces
- Sea Salt & Black Pepper to Taste
- 1/4 Cup Dry White Wine
- 1/4 Cup Seafood Stock
- 2 Cloves Garlic, Minced
- 1 Bay Leaf
- 1/2 Teaspoon Sage, Fresh & Chopped
- 2 Rosemary Sprigs to Garnish

Directions:

Start by turning your oven to 375, and then season the fillets with salt and pepper. Place them in a baking pan, and add in your stock, garlic, wine, sage and bay leaf. Cover well, and then bake for twenty minutes. Your fish should be flaky when tested with a fork.

Use a spatula to remove each fillet, placing the liquid over high heat and cooking to reduce in half. This should take ten minutes, and you need to stir frequently. Serve dripped in poaching liquid and garnished with a rosemary sprig.

Nutrition (for 100g): 361 calories 10g fats 9g carbohydrates 34g protein 783mg sodium

Mussels in White Wine

Preparation Time : 5 minutes

Cooking Time : 10 minutes

Servings : 2

Difficulty Level : Difficult

Ingredients:

- 2 lbs. Live Mussels, Fresh
- 1 Cup Dry White Wine
- 1/4 Teaspoon Sea Salt, Fine
- 3 Cloves Garlic, Minced
- 2 Teaspoons Shallots, Diced
- 1/4 Cup Parsley, Fresh & Chopped, Divided
- 2 Tablespoons olive Oil
- 1/4 Lemon, Juiced

Directions:

Get out a colander and scrub your mussels, rinsing them using cold water. Discard mussels that will not close if they're tapped, and then use a paring knife to remove the beard from each one.

Get out stockpot, placing it over medium-high heat, and add in your garlic, shallots, wine and parsley. Bring it to a simmer. Once it's at a steady simmer, add in your mussels and cover. Allow them to simmer for five to seven minutes. Make sure they do not overcook.

Use a slotted spoon to remove them, and add your lemon juice and olive oil into the pot. Stir well, and pour the broth over your mussels before serving with parsley.

Nutrition (for 100g): 345 calories 9g fats 18g carbohydrates 37g protein 693mg sodium

Dilly Salmon

Preparation Time : 10 minutes

Cooking Time : 15 minutes

Servings : 2

Difficulty Level : Average

Ingredients:

- 2 Salmon Fillets, 6 Ounces Each
- 1 Tablespoon Olive Oil
- 1/2 Tangerine, Juiced
- 2 Teaspoons Orange Zest
- 2 Tablespoons Dill, Fresh & Chopped
- Sea Salt & Black Pepper to Taste

Directions:

Prepare oven to 375 degrees, and then get out two ten-inch pieces of foil. Rub your filets down with olive oil on both side before seasoning with salt and pepper, placing each fillet into a piece of foil.

Drizzle your orange juice over each one, and then top with orange zest and dill. Fold your packet closed, making sure it has two inches of air space within the foil so your fish can steam, and then place them on a baking dish.

Bake for fifteen minutes before opening the packets, and transfer to two serving plates. Pour the sauce over the top of each before serving.

Nutrition (for 100g): 366 calories 14g fats 9g carbohydrates 36g protein 689mg sodium

Smooth Salmon

Preparation Time : 8 minutes

Cooking Time : 8 minutes

Servings : 2

Difficulty Level : Easy

Ingredients:

- Salmon, 6-ounce fillet
- Lemon, 2 slices
- Capers, 1 tablespoon
- Sea salt and pepper, 1/8 teaspoon
- Extra virgin olive oil, 1 tablespoon

Directions:

Place a clean skillet over a medium heat to prepare for 3 minutes. Place olive oil on a plate, and coat the salmon completely. Cook the salmon over a high heat in the skillet.

Top the salmon with the rest of the ingredients, and turn to cook each side. Notice when both sides are brown. It may take 3-5 minutes each side. Make sure the salmon is cooked by testing with a fork.

Serve with lemon slices.

Nutrition (for 100g): 371 Calories 25.1g Fat 0.9g Carbohydrates 33.7g Protein 782mg Sodium

Tuna Melody

Preparation Time : 20 minutes

Cooking Time : 20 minutes

Servings : 2

Difficulty Level : Easy

Ingredients:

- Tuna, 12 ounces
- Green onions, 1 for garnish
- Bell pepper, ¼, chopped
- Vinegar, 1 dash
- Salt and pepper to taste
- Avocados, 1, halved and pitted
- Greek yogurt, 2 tablespoons

Directions:

Mix the tuna with the vinegar, onion, yogurt, avocado and pepper in a bowl.

Add the seasonings, mix, and serve with the green onion garnish.

Nutrition (for 100g): 294 Calories 19g Fat 10g Carbohydrates 12g Protein 836mg Sodium

Sea Cheese

Preparation Time : 12 minutes

Cooking Time : 25 minutes

Servings : 2

Difficulty Level : Easy

Ingredients:

- Salmon, 6-ounce fillet
- Dried basil, 1 tablespoon
- Cheese, 2 tablespoons, grated
- Tomato, 1, sliced
- Extra virgin olive oil, 1 tablespoon

Directions:

Prepare a baking oven at 375 F. Layer aluminum foil in a baking dish, and spray with cooking oil. Carefully transfer the salmon to the baking tray and top with the rest of the ingredients.

Let the salmon brown for 20 minutes. Allow to cool for five minutes, and transfer to a serving plate. You will see the topping in the middle of the salmon.

Nutrition (for 100g): 411 Calories 26.6g Fat 1.6g Carbohydrates 8g Protein 822mg Sodium

Healthy Steaks

Preparation Time : 10 minutes

Cooking Time : 20 minutes

Servings : 2

Difficulty Level : Easy

Ingredients:

- Olive oil, 1 teaspoon
- Halibut steak, 8 ounces
- Garlic, ½ teaspoon, minced
- Butter, 1 tablespoon
- Salt and pepper to taste

Directions:

Heat a skillet and add the oil. Over a medium flame, brown the steaks in a pan, melt the butter with the garlic, salt and pepper. Add the steaks, toss to coat, and serve.

Nutrition (for 100g): 284 Calories 17g Fat 0.2g Carbohydrates 8g Protein 755mg Sodium

Herbal Salmon

Preparation Time : 8 minutes

Cooking Time : 18 minutes

Servings : 2

Difficulty Level : Easy

Ingredients:

- Salmon, 2 fillets without skin
- Coarse salt to taste
- Extra virgin olive oil, 1 tablespoon
- Lemon, 1, sliced
- Fresh rosemary, 4 sprigs

Directions:

Preheat the oven to 400F. Situate aluminum foil in a baking dish, and place salmon on top. Top the salmon with the rest of the ingredients and bake for 20 minutes. Serve immediately with lemon slices.

Nutrition (for 100g): 257 Calories 18g Fat 2.7g Carbohydrates 7g Protein 836mg Sodium

Smokey Glazed Tuna

Preparation Time : 35 minutes

Cooking Time : 10 minutes

Servings : 2

Difficulty Level : Easy

Ingredients:

- Tuna, 4-ounce steaks
- Orange juice, 1 tablespoon
- Minced garlic, ½ clove
- Lemon juice, ½ teaspoon
- Fresh parsley, 1 tablespoon, chopped
- Soy sauce, 1 tablespoon
- Extra virgin olive oil, 1 tablespoon
- Ground black pepper, ¼ teaspoon
- Oregano, ¼ teaspoon

Directions:

Pick a mixing dish, and add all the ingredients, except the tuna. Mix well, and then add the tuna to marinade. Refrigerate this mixture for half an hour. Heat a grill pan and cook the tuna on each side for 5 minutes. Serve when cooked.

Nutrition (for 100g): 200 Calories 7.9g Fat 0.3g Carbohydrates 10g Protein 734mg Sodium

Crusty Halibut

Preparation Time : 20 minutes

Cooking Time : 15 minutes

Servings : 2

Difficulty Level : Easy

Ingredients:

- Parsley to top
- Fresh dill, 2 tablespoons, chopped
- Fresh chives, 2 tablespoons, chopped
- Olive oil, 1 tablespoon
- Salt and pepper to taste
- Halibut, fillets, 6 ounces
- Lemon zest, ½ teaspoon, finely grated
- Greek yogurt, 2 tablespoons

Directions:

Preheat the oven to 400F. Line a baking sheet with foil. Add all the ingredients to a wide dish, and marinate the fillets. Rinse and dry the fillets; then add to the oven and bake for 15 minutes.

Nutrition (for 100g): 273 Calories 7.2g Fat 0.4g Carbohydrates 9g Protein 783mg Sodium

Fit Tuna

Preparation Time : 15 minutes

Cooking Time : 10 minutes

Servings : 2

Difficulty Level : Easy

Ingredients:

- Egg, ½
- Onion, 1 tablespoon, finely chopped
- Celery to top
- Salt and pepper to taste
- Garlic, 1 clove, minced
- Canned tuna, 7 ounces
- Greek yogurt, 2 tablespoons

Directions:

Drain the tuna, and add the egg and yogurt with the garlic, salt and pepper.

In a bowl, combine this mixture with onions and shape into patties. Take a large skillet and brown the patties for 3 minutes per side. Drain and serve.

Nutrition (for 100g): 230 Calories 13g Fat 0.8g Carbohydrates 10g Protein 866mg Sodium

Hot and Fresh Fishy Steaks

Preparation Time : 14 minutes

Cooking Time : 14 minutes

Servings : 2

Difficulty Level : Easy

Ingredients:

- Garlic, 1 clove, minced
- Lemon juice, 1 tablespoon
- Brown sugar, 1 tablespoon
- Halibut steak, 1 pound
- Salt and pepper to taste
- Soy sauce, ¼ teaspoon
- Butter, 1 teaspoon
- Greek yogurt, 2 tablespoons

Directions:

Over a medium flame, preheat the grill. Mix the butter, sugar, yogurt, lemon juice, soy sauce and seasonings in a bowl. Warm the mixture in a pan. Use this mixture to brush onto the steak while cooking on the griller. Serve hot.

Nutrition (for 100g): 412 Calories 19.4g Fat 7.6g Carbohydrates 11g Protein 788mg Sodium

Mussels O' Marine

Preparation Time : 20 minutes

Cooking Time : 10 minutes

Servings : 2

Difficulty Level : Easy

Ingredients:

- Mussels, scrubbed and debearded, 1 pound
- Coconut milk, ½ cup
- Cayenne pepper, 1 teaspoon
- Fresh lemon juice, 1 tablespoon
- Garlic, 1 teaspoon, minced
- Cilantro, freshly chopped for topping
- Brown sugar, 1 teaspoon

Directions:

Mix all the ingredients, except the mussels in a pot. Heat the mixture and bring it to the boil. Add the mussels, and cook for 10 minutes. Serve in a dish with the boiled liquid.

Nutrition (for 100g): 483 Calories 24.4g Fat 21.6g Carbohydrates 1.2g Protein 499mg Sodium

Slow Cooker Mediterranean Beef Roast

Preparation Time : 10 minutes

Cooking Time : 10 hours and 10 minutes

Servings : 6

Difficulty Level : Average

Ingredients:

- 3 pounds Chuck roast, boneless
- 2 teaspoons Rosemary
- ½ cup Tomatoes, sun-dried and chopped
- 10 cloves Grated garlic
- ½ cup Beef stock
- 2 tablespoons Balsamic vinegar
- ¼ cup Chopped Italian parsley, fresh
- ¼ cup Chopped olives
- 1 teaspoon Lemon zest
- ¼ cup Cheese grits

Directions:

In the slow cooker, put garlic, sun dried tomatoes, and the beef roast. Add beef stock and Rosemary. Close the cooker and slow cook for 10 hours.

After cooking is over, remove the beef, and shred the meet. Discard the fat. Add back the shredded meat to the slow cooker and simmer for 10 minutes. In a small bowl combine lemon zest, parsley, and olives. Cool the mixture until you are ready to serve. Garnish using the refrigerated mix.

Serve it over pasta or egg noodles. Top it with cheese grits.

Nutrition (for 100g): 314 Calories 19g Fat 1g Carbohydrate 32g Protein 778mg Sodium

Slow Cooker Mediterranean Beef with Artichokes

Preparation Time : 3 hours and 20 minutes

Cooking Time : 7 hours and 8 minutes

Servings : 6

Difficulty Level : Easy

Ingredients:

- 2 pounds Beef for stew
- 14 ounces Artichoke hearts
- 1 tablespoon Grape seed oil
- 1 Diced onion
- 32 ounces Beef broth
- 4 cloves Garlic, grated
- 14½ ounces Tinned tomatoes, diced
- 15 ounces Tomato sauce
- 1 teaspoon Dried oregano
- ½ cup Pitted, chopped olives
- 1 teaspoon Dried parsley
- 1 teaspoon Dried oregano
- ½ teaspoon Ground cumin
- 1 teaspoon Dried basil
- 1 Bay leaf
- ½ teaspoon Salt

Directions:

In a large non-stick skillet pour some oil and bring to medium-high heat. Roast the beef until it turns brown on both the sides. Transfer the beef into a slow cooker.

Add in beef broth, diced tomatoes, tomato sauce, salt and combine. Pour in beef broth, diced tomatoes, oregano, olives, basil, parsley, bay leaf, and cumin. Combine the mixture thoroughly.

Close and cook on low heat for 7 hours. Discard the bay leaf at the time serving. Serve hot.

Nutrition (for 100g): 416 Calories 5g Fat 14.1g Carbohydrates 29.9g Protein 811mg Sodium

Skinny Slow Cooker Mediterranean Style Pot Roast

Preparation Time : 30 minutes

Cooking Time : 8 hours

Servings : 10

Difficulty Level : Difficult

Ingredients:

- 4 pounds Eye of round roast
- 4 cloves Garlic
- 2 teaspoons Olive oil
- 1 teaspoon Freshly ground black pepper
- 1 cup Chopped onions
- 4 Carrots, chopped
- 2 teaspoons Dried Rosemary
- 2 Chopped celery stalks
- 28 ounces Crushed tomatoes in the can
- 1 cup Low sodium beef broth
- 1 cup Red wine
- 2 teaspoons Salt

Directions:

Season the beef roast with salt, garlic, and pepper and set aside. Pour oil in a non-stick skillet and bring to medium-high heat. Put the beef into it and roast until it becomes brown on all sides. Now, transfer the roasted beef into a 6-quart slow cooker. Add carrots, onion, rosemary, and celery into the skillet. Continue cooking until the onion and vegetable become soft.

Stir in the tomatoes and wine into this vegetable mixture. Add beef broth and tomato mixture into the slow cooker along with the vegetable mixture. Close and cook on low for 8 hours.

Once the meat gets cooked, remove it from the slow cooker and place it on a cutting board and wrap with an aluminum foil. To thicken the sauce, then transfer it into a saucepan and boil it under low heat until it reaches to the required consistency. Discard fats before serving.

Nutrition (for 100g): 260 Calories 6g Fat 8.7g Carbohydrates 37.6g Protein 588mg Sodium

Slow Cooker Meatloaf

Preparation Time : 10 minutes

Cooking Time : 6 hours and 10 minutes

Servings : 8

Difficulty Level : Average

Ingredients:

- 2 pounds Ground bison
- 1 Grated zucchini
- 2 large Eggs
- Olive oil cooking spray as required
- 1 Zucchini, shredded
- ½ cup Parsley, fresh, finely chopped
- ½ cup Parmesan cheese, shredded
- 3 tablespoons Balsamic vinegar
- 4 Garlic cloves, grated
- 2 tablespoons Onion minced
- 1 tablespoon Dried oregano
- ½ teaspoon Ground black pepper
- ½ teaspoon Kosher salt
- For the topping:
- ¼ cup Shredded Mozzarella cheese
- ¼ cup Ketchup without sugar
- ¼ cup Freshly chopped parsley

Directions:

Stripe line the inside of a six-quart slow cooker with aluminum foil. Spray non-stick cooking oil over it.

In a large bowl combine ground bison or extra lean ground sirloin, zucchini, eggs, parsley, balsamic vinegar, garlic, dried oregano, sea or kosher salt, minced dry onion, and ground black pepper.

Situate this mixture into the slow cooker and form an oblong shaped loaf. Cover the cooker, set on a low heat and cook for 6 hours. After cooking, open the cooker and spread ketchup all over the meatloaf.

Now, place the cheese above the ketchup as a new layer and close the slow cooker. Let the meatloaf sit on these two layers for about 10 minutes or until the cheese starts to melt. Garnish with fresh parsley, and shredded Mozzarella cheese.

Nutrition (for 100g): 320 Calories 2g Fat 4g Carbohydrates 26g Protein 681mg Sodium

Slow Cooker Mediterranean Beef Hoagies

Preparation Time : 10 minutes

Cooking Time : 13 hours

Servings : 6

Difficulty Level : Average

Ingredients:

- 3 pounds Beef top round roast fatless
- ½ teaspoon Onion powder
- ½ teaspoon Black pepper
- 3 cups Low sodium beef broth
- 4 teaspoons Salad dressing mix
- 1 Bay leaf
- 1 tablespoon Garlic, minced
- 2 Red bell peppers, thin strips cut
- 16 ounces Pepperoncino
- 8 slices Sargento Provolone, thin
- 2 ounces Gluten-free bread
- ½ teaspoon salt
- For seasoning:
- 1½ tablespoon Onion powder
- 1½ tablespoon Garlic powder
- 2 tablespoon Dried parsley
- 1 tablespoon stevia
- ½ teaspoon Dried thyme

- 1 tablespoon Dried oregano
- 2 tablespoons Black pepper
- 1 tablespoon Salt
- 6 Cheese slices

Directions:

Dry the roast with a paper towel. Combine black pepper, onion powder and salt in a small bowl and rub the mixture over the roast. Place the seasoned roast into a slow cooker.

Add broth, salad dressing mix, bay leaf, and garlic to the slow cooker. Combine it gently. Close and set to low cooking for 12 hours. After cooking, remove the bay leaf.

Take out the cooked beef and shred the beef meet. Put back the shredded beef and add bell peppers and. Add bell peppers and pepperoncino into the slow cooker. Cover the cooker and low cook for 1 hour. Before serving, top each of the bread with 3 ounces of the meat mixture. Top it with a cheese slice. The liquid gravy can be used as a dip.

Nutrition (for 100g): 442 Calories 11.5g Fat 37g Carbohydrates 49g Protein 735mg Sodium

Mediterranean Pork Roast

Preparation Time : 10 minutes

Cooking Time : 8 hours and 10 minutes

Servings : 6

Difficulty Level : Average

Ingredients:

- 2 tablespoons Olive oil
- 2 pounds Pork roast
- ½ teaspoon Paprika
- ¾ cup Chicken broth
- 2 teaspoons Dried sage
- ½ tablespoon Garlic minced
- ¼ teaspoon Dried marjoram
- ¼ teaspoon Dried Rosemary
- 1 teaspoon Oregano
- ¼ teaspoon Dried thyme
- 1 teaspoon Basil
- ¼ teaspoon Kosher salt

Directions:

In a small bowl mix broth, oil, salt, and spices. In a skillet pour olive oil and bring to medium-high heat. Put the pork into it and roast until all sides become brown.

Take out the pork after cooking and poke the roast all over with a knife. Place the poked pork roast into a 6-quart crock pot. Now, pour the small bowl mixture liquid all over the roast.

Seal crock pot and cook on low for 8 hours. After cooking, remove it from the crock pot on to a cutting board and shred into pieces. Afterward, add the shredded pork back into the crockpot. Simmer it another 10 minutes. Serve along with feta cheese, pita bread, and tomatoes.

Nutrition (for 100g): 361 Calories 10.4g Fat 0.7g Carbohydrates 43.8g Protein 980mg Sodium

Beef Pizza

Preparation Time : 20 minutes

Cooking Time : 50 minutes

Servings : 10

Difficulty Level : Difficult

Ingredients:

- For Crust:
- 3 cups all-purpose flour
- 1 tablespoon sugar
- 2¼ teaspoons active dry yeast
- 1 teaspoon salt
- 2 tablespoons olive oil
- 1 cup warm water
- For Topping:
- 1-pound ground beef
- 1 medium onion, chopped
- 2 tablespoons tomato paste
- 1 tablespoon ground cumin
- Salt and ground black pepper, as required
- ¼ cup water
- 1 cup fresh spinach, chopped
- 8 ounces artichoke hearts, quartered
- 4 ounces fresh mushrooms, sliced

- 2 tomatoes, chopped
- 4 ounces feta cheese, crumbled

Directions:

For crust:

Mix the flour, sugar, yeast and salt with a stand mixer, using the dough hook. Add 2 tablespoons of the oil and warm water and knead until a smooth and elastic dough is formed.

Make a ball of the dough and set aside for about 15 minutes.

Situate the dough onto a lightly floured surface and roll into a circle. Situate the dough into a lightly, greased round pizza pan and gently, press to fit. Set aside for about 10-15 minutes. Coat the crust with some oil. Preheat the oven to 400 degrees F.

For topping:

Fry beef in a nonstick skillet over medium-high heat for about 4-5 minutes. Mix in the onion and cook for about 5 minutes, stirring frequently. Add the tomato paste, cumin, salt, black pepper and water and stir to combine.

Set the heat to medium and cook for about 5-10 minutes. Remove from the heat and set aside. Place the beef mixture over the pizza crust and top with the spinach, followed by the artichokes, mushrooms, tomatoes, and Feta cheese.

Bake until the cheese is melted. Remove from the oven and set aside for about 3-5 minutes before slicing. Cut into desired sized slices and serve.

Nutrition (for 100g): 309 Calories 8.7g Fat 3.7g Carbohydrates 3.3g Protein 732mg Sodium

Beef & Bulgur Meatballs

Preparation Time : 20 minutes

Cooking Time : 28 minutes

Servings : 6

Difficulty Level : Average

Ingredients:

- ¾ cup uncooked bulgur
- 1-pound ground beef
- ¼ cup shallots, minced
- ¼ cup fresh parsley, minced
- ½ teaspoon ground allspice
- ½ teaspoon ground cumin
- ½ teaspoon ground cinnamon
- ¼ teaspoon red pepper flakes, crushed
- Salt, as required
- 1 tablespoon olive oil

Directions:

In a large bowl of the cold water, soak the bulgur for about 30 minutes. Drain the bulgur well and then, squeeze with your hands to remove the excess water. In a food processor, add the bulgur, beef, shallot, parsley, spices, salt, and pulse until a smooth mixture is formed.

Situate the mixture into a bowl and refrigerate, covered for about 30 minutes. Remove from the refrigerator and make equal sized balls from the beef mixture. In a large nonstick skillet, heat the oil over medium-high heat and cook the meatballs in 2 batches for about 13-14 minutes, flipping frequently. Serve warm.

Nutrition (for 100g): 228 Calories 7.4g Fat 0.1g Carbohydrates 3.5g Protein 766mg Sodium

Tasty Beef and Broccoli

Preparation Time : 10 minutes

Cooking Time : 15 minutes

Servings : 4

Difficulty Level : Easy

Ingredients:

- 1 and ½ lbs. flanks steak
- 1 tbsp. olive oil
- 1 tbsp. tamari sauce
- 1 cup beef stock
- 1-pound broccoli, florets separated

Directions:

Combine steak strips with oil and tamari, toss and set aside for 10 minutes. Select your instant pot on sauté mode, place beef strips and brown them for 4 minutes on each side. Stir in stock, cover the pot again and cook on high for 8 minutes. Stir in broccoli, cover and cook on high for 4 minutes more. Portion everything between plates and serve. Enjoy!

Nutrition (for 100g): 312 Calories 5g Fat 20g Carbohydrates 4g Protein 694mg Sodium

Beef Corn Chili

Preparation Time : 8-10 minutes

Cooking Time : 30 minutes

Servings : 8

Difficulty Level : Average

Ingredients:

- 2 small onions, chopped (finely)
- ¼ cup canned corn
- 1 tablespoon oil
- 10 ounces lean ground beef
- 2 small chili peppers, diced

Directions:

Turn on the instant pot. Click "SAUTE". Pour the oil then stir in the onions, chili pepper, and beef; cook until turn translucent and softened. Pour the 3 cups water in the Cooking pot; mix well.

Seal the lid. Select "MEAT/STEW". Adjust the timer to 20 minutes. Allow to cook until the timer turns to zero.

Click "CANCEL" then "NPR" for natural release pressure for about 8-10 minutes. Open then place the dish in serving plates. Serve.

Nutrition (for 100g): 94 Calories 5g Fat 2g Carbohydrates 7g Protein 477mg Sodium

Balsamic Beef Dish

Preparation Time : 5 minutes

Cooking Time : 55 minutes

Servings : 8

Difficulty Level : Average

Ingredients:

- 3 pounds chuck roast
- 3 cloves garlic, thinly sliced
- 1 tablespoon oil
- 1 teaspoon flavored vinegar
- ½ teaspoon pepper
- ½ teaspoon rosemary
- 1 tablespoon butter
- ½ teaspoon thyme
- ¼ cup balsamic vinegar
- 1 cup beef broth

Directions:

Slice the slits in the roast and stuff in garlic slices all over. Combine flavored vinegar, rosemary, pepper, thyme and rub the mixture over the roast. Select the pot on sauté mode and mix in oil, allow the oil to heat up. Cook both side of the roast.

Take it out and set aside. Stir in butter, broth, balsamic vinegar and deglaze the pot. Return the roast and close the lid, then cook on HIGH pressure for 40 minutes.

Perform a quick release. Serve!

Nutrition (for 100g): 393 Calories 15g Fat 25g Carbohydrates 37g Protein 870mg Sodium

Soy Sauce Beef Roast

Preparation Time : 8 minutes

Cooking Time : 35 minutes

Servings : 2-3

Difficulty Level : Average

Ingredients:

- ½ teaspoon beef bouillon
- 1 ½ teaspoon rosemary
- ½ teaspoon minced garlic
- 2 pounds roast beef
- 1/3 cup soy sauce

Directions:

Combine the soy sauce, bouillon, rosemary, and garlic together in a mixing bowl.

Turn on your instant pot. Place the roast, and pour enough water to cover the roast; gently stir to mix well. Seal it tight.

Click "MEAT/STEW" Cooking function; set pressure level to "HIGH" and set the Cooking time to 35 minutes. Let the pressure to build to cook the ingredients. Once done, click "CANCEL" setting then click "NPR" Cooking function to release the pressure naturally.

Gradually open the lid, and shred the meat. Mix in the shredded meat back in the potting mix and stir well. Transfer in serving containers. Serve warm.

Nutrition (for 100g): 423 Calories 14g Fat 12g Carbohydrates 21g Protein 884mg Sodium

Rosemary Beef Chuck Roast

Preparation Time : 5 minutes

Cooking Time : 45 minutes

Servings : 5-6

Difficulty Level : Average

Ingredients:

- 3 pounds chuck beef roast
- 3 garlic cloves
- ¼ cup balsamic vinegar
- 1 sprig fresh rosemary
- 1 sprig fresh thyme
- 1 cup of water
- 1 tablespoon vegetable oil
- Salt and pepper to taste

Directions:

Chop slices in the beef roast and place the garlic cloves in them. Rub the roast with the herbs, black pepper, and salt. Preheat your instant pot using the sauté setting and pour the oil. When warmed, mix in the beef roast and stir-cook until browned on all sides. Add the remaining ingredients; stir gently.

Seal tight and cook on high for 40 minutes using manual setting. Allow the pressure release naturally, about 10 minutes. Uncover and put the beef roast the serving plates, slice and serve.

Nutrition (for 100g): 542 Calories 11.2g Fat 8.7g Carbohydrates 55.2g Protein 710mg Sodium

Pork Chops and Tomato Sauce

Preparation Time : 10 minutes

Cooking Time : 20 minutes

Servings : 4

Difficulty Level : Easy

Ingredients:

- 4 pork chops, boneless
- 1 tablespoon soy sauce
- ¼ teaspoon sesame oil
- 1 and ½ cups tomato paste
- 1 yellow onion
- 8 mushrooms, sliced

Directions:

In a bowl, mix pork chops with soy sauce and sesame oil, toss and leave aside for 10 minutes. Set your instant pot on sauté mode, add pork chops and brown them for 5 minutes on each side. Stir in onion, and cook for 1-2 minutes more. Add tomato paste and mushrooms, toss, cover and cook on high for 8-9 minutes. Divide everything between plates and serve. Enjoy!

Nutrition (for 100g): 300 Calories 7g Fat 18g Carbohydrates 4g Protein 801mg Sodium

Chicken with Caper Sauce

Preparation Time : 10 minutes

Cooking Time : 18 minutes

Servings : 5

Difficulty Level : Difficult

Ingredients:

- <u>For Chicken:</u>
- 2 eggs
- Salt and ground black pepper, as required
- 1 cup dry breadcrumbs
- 2 tablespoons olive oil
- 1½ pounds skinless, boneless chicken breast halves, pounded into ¾inch thickness and cut into pieces
- <u>For Capers Sauce:</u>
- 3 tablespoons capers
- ½ cup dry white wine
- 3 tablespoons fresh lemon juice
- Salt and ground black pepper, as required
- 2 tablespoons fresh parsley, chopped

Directions:

For chicken: in a shallow dish, add the eggs, salt and black pepper and beat until well combined. In another shallow dish, place breadcrumbs. Soak the chicken pieces in egg mixture then coat with the breadcrumbs evenly. Shake off the excess breadcrumbs.

Cook the oil over medium heat and cook the chicken pieces for about 5-7 minutes per side or until desired doneness. With a slotted spoon, situate the chicken pieces onto a paper towel lined plate. With a piece of the foil, cover the chicken pieces to keep them warm.

In the same skillet, incorporate all the sauce ingredients except parsley and cook for about 2-3 minutes, stirring continuously. Mix in the parsley and remove from heat. Serve the chicken pieces with the topping of capers sauce.

Nutrition (for 100g): 352 Calories 13.5g Fat 1.9g Carbohydrates 1.2g Protein 741mg Sodium

Turkey Burgers with Mango Salsa

Preparation Time : 15 minutes

Cooking Time : 10 minutes

Servings : 6

Difficulty Level : Easy

Ingredients:

- 1½ pounds ground turkey breast
- 1 teaspoon sea salt, divided
- ¼ teaspoon freshly ground black pepper
- 2 tablespoons extra-virgin olive oil
- 2 mangos, peeled, pitted, and cubed
- ½ red onion, finely chopped
- Juice of 1 lime
- 1 garlic clove, minced
- ½ jalapeño pepper, seeded and finely minced
- 2 tablespoons chopped fresh cilantro leaves

Directions:

Form the turkey breast into 4 patties and season with ½ teaspoon of sea salt and the pepper. Cook the olive oil in a nonstick skillet until it shimmers. Add the turkey patties and cook for about 5 minutes per side until browned. While the patties cook, mix the mango, red onion, lime juice, garlic, jalapeño, cilantro, and remaining ½ teaspoon of sea salt in a small bowl. Spoon the salsa over the turkey patties and serve.

Nutrition (for 100g): 384 Calories 3g Fat 27g Carbohydrates 34g Protein 692mg Sodium

Herb-Roasted Turkey Breast

Preparation Time : 15 minutes

Cooking Time : 1½ hours (plus 20 minutes to rest)

Servings : 6

Difficulty Level : Average

Ingredients:

- 2 tablespoons extra-virgin olive oil
- 4 garlic cloves, minced
- Zest of 1 lemon
- 1 tablespoon chopped fresh thyme leaves
- 1 tablespoon chopped fresh rosemary leaves
- 2 tablespoons chopped fresh Italian parsley leaves
- 1 teaspoon ground mustard
- 1 teaspoon sea salt
- ¼ teaspoon freshly ground black pepper
- 1 (6-pound) bone-in, skin-on turkey breast
- 1 cup dry white wine

Directions:

Preheat the oven to 325°F. Combine the olive oil, garlic, lemon zest, thyme, rosemary, parsley, mustard, sea salt, and pepper. Brush the herb mixture evenly over the surface of the turkey breast, and loosen the skin and rub underneath as well. Situate the turkey breast in a roasting pan on a rack, skin-side up.

Pour the wine in the pan. Roast for 1 to 1½ hours until the turkey reaches an internal temperature of 165 degrees F. Pull out from the oven and set separately for 20 minutes, tented with aluminum foil to keep it warm, before carving.

Nutrition (for 100g): 392 Calories 1g Fat 2g Carbohydrates 84g Protein 741mg Sodium

Chicken Sausage and Peppers

Preparation Time : 10 minutes

Cooking Time : 20 minutes

Servings : 6

Difficulty Level : Average

Ingredients:

- 2 tablespoons extra-virgin olive oil
- 6 Italian chicken sausage links
- 1 onion
- 1 red bell pepper
- 1 green bell pepper
- 3 garlic cloves, minced
- ½ cup dry white wine
- ½ teaspoon sea salt
- ¼ teaspoon freshly ground black pepper
- Pinch red pepper flakes

Directions:

Cook the olive oil on large skillet until it shimmers. Add the sausages and cook for 5 to 7 minutes, turning occasionally, until browned, and they reach an internal temperature of 165°F. With tongs, remove the sausage from the pan and set aside on a platter, tented with aluminum foil to keep warm.

Return the skillet to the heat and mix in the onion, red bell pepper, and green bell pepper. Cook and stir occasionally, until the vegetables begin to brown. Put in the garlic and cook for 30 seconds, stirring constantly.

Stir in the wine, sea salt, pepper, and red pepper flakes. Pull out and fold in any browned bits from the bottom of the pan. Simmer for about 4 minutes more, stirring, until the liquid reduces by half. Spoon the peppers over the sausages and serve.

Nutrition (for 100g): 173 Calories 1g Fat 6g Carbohydrates 22g Protein 582mg Sodium

Chicken Piccata

Preparation Time : 10 minutes

Cooking Time : 15 minutes

Servings : 6

Difficulty Level : Average

Ingredients:

- ½ cup whole-wheat flour
- ½ teaspoon sea salt
- 1/8 teaspoon freshly ground black pepper
- 1½ pounds chicken breasts, cut into 6 pieces
- 3 tablespoons extra-virgin olive oil
- 1 cup unsalted chicken broth
- ½ cup dry white wine
- Juice of 1 lemon
- Zest of 1 lemon
- ¼ cup capers, drained and rinsed
- ¼ cup chopped fresh parsley leaves

Directions:

In a shallow dish, whisk the flour, sea salt, and pepper. Scour the chicken in the flour and tap off any excess. Cook the olive oil until it shimmers.

Put the chicken and cook for about 4 minutes per side until browned. Pull out the chicken from the pan and set aside, tented with aluminum foil to keep warm.

Situate the skillet back to the heat and stir in the broth, wine, lemon juice, lemon zest, and capers. Use the side of a spoon scoop and fold in any browned bits from the pan's bottom. Simmer until the liquid thickens. Take out the skillet from the heat and take the chicken back to the pan. Turn to coat. Stir in the parsley and serve.

Nutrition (for 100g): 153 Calories 2g Fat 9g Carbohydrates 8g Protein 692mg Sodium

One-Pan Tuscan Chicken

Preparation Time : 10 minutes

Cooking Time : 25 minutes

Servings : 6

Difficulty Level : Difficult

Ingredients:

- ¼ cup extra-virgin olive oil, divided
- 1-pound boneless, skinless chicken breasts, cut into ¾-inch pieces
- 1 onion, chopped
- 1 red bell pepper, chopped
- 3 garlic cloves, minced
- ½ cup dry white wine
- 1 (14-ounce) can crushed tomatoes, undrained
- 1 (14-ounce) can chopped tomatoes, drained
- 1 (14-ounce) can white beans, drained
- 1 tablespoon dried Italian seasoning
- ½ teaspoon sea salt
- 1/8 teaspoon freshly ground black pepper
- 1/8 teaspoon red pepper flakes
- ¼ cup chopped fresh basil leaves

Directions:

Cook 2 tablespoons of olive oil until it shimmers. Mix in the chicken and cook until browned. Remove the chicken from the skillet and set aside on a platter, tented with aluminum foil to keep warm.

Situate the skillet back to the heat and heat up the remaining olive oil. Add the onion and red bell pepper. Cook and stir rarely, until the vegetables are soft. Put the garlic and cook for 30 seconds, stirring constantly.

Stir in the wine, and use the side of the spoon to scoop out any browned bits from the bottom of the pan. Cook for 1 minute, stirring.

Mix in the crushed and chopped tomatoes, white beans, Italian seasoning, sea salt, pepper, and red pepper flakes. Allow to simmer. Cook for 5 minutes, stirring occasionally.

Put the chicken back and any juices that have collected to the skillet. Cook until the chicken is cook through. Take out from the heat and stir in the basil before serving.

Nutrition (for 100g): 271 Calories 8g Fat 29g Carbohydrates 14g Protein 596mg Sodium

Chicken Kapama

Preparation Time : 10 minutes

Cooking Time : 2 hours

Servings : 4

Difficulty Level : Average

Ingredients:

- 1 (32-ounce) can chopped tomatoes, drained
- ¼ cup dry white wine
- 2 tablespoons tomato paste
- 3 tablespoons extra-virgin olive oil
- ¼ teaspoon red pepper flakes
- 1 teaspoon ground allspice
- ½ teaspoon dried oregano
- 2 whole cloves
- 1 cinnamon stick
- ½ teaspoon sea salt
- 1/8 teaspoon freshly ground black pepper
- 4 boneless, skinless chicken breast halves

Directions:

Mix the tomatoes, wine, tomato paste, olive oil, red pepper flakes, allspice, oregano, cloves, cinnamon stick, sea salt, and pepper in large pot. Bring to a simmer, stirring occasionally. Allow to simmer for 30 minutes, stirring occasionally. Remove and discard the whole cloves and cinnamon stick from the sauce and let the sauce cool.

Preheat the oven to 350°F. Situate the chicken in a 9-by-13-inch baking dish. Pour the sauce over the chicken and cover the pan with aluminum foil. Continue baking until it reaches 165°F internal temperature.

Nutrition (for 100g): 220 Calories 3g Fat 11g Carbohydrates 8g Protein 923mg Sodium

Spinach and Feta–Stuffed Chicken Breasts

Preparation Time : 10 minutes

Cooking Time : 45 minutes

Servings : 4

Difficulty Level : Average

Ingredients:

- 2 tablespoons extra-virgin olive oil
- 1-pound fresh baby spinach
- 3 garlic cloves, minced
- Zest of 1 lemon
- ½ teaspoon sea salt
- 1/8 teaspoon freshly ground black pepper
- ½ cup crumbled feta cheese
- 4 boneless, skinless chicken breasts

Directions:

Preheat the oven to 350°F. Cook the olive oil over medium heat until it shimmers. Add the spinach. Continue cooking and stirring, until wilted.

Stir in the garlic, lemon zest, sea salt, and pepper. Cook for 30 seconds, stirring constantly. Cool slightly and mix in the cheese.

Spread the spinach and cheese mixture in an even layer over the chicken pieces and roll the breast around the filling. Hold closed with toothpicks or butcher's twine. Place the breasts in a 9-by-13-

inch baking dish and bake for 30 to 40 minutes, or until the chicken have an internal temperature of 165°F. Take out from the oven and set aside for 5 minutes before slicing and serving.

Nutrition (for 100g): 263 Calories 3g Fat 7g Carbohydrates 17g Protein 639mg Sodium

Rosemary Baked Chicken Drumsticks

Preparation Time : 5 minutes

Cooking Time : 1 hour

Servings : 6

Difficulty Level : Easy

Ingredients:

- 2 tablespoons chopped fresh rosemary leaves
- 1 teaspoon garlic powder
- ½ teaspoon sea salt
- 1/8 teaspoon freshly ground black pepper
- Zest of 1 lemon
- 12 chicken drumsticks

Directions:

Preheat the oven to 350°F. Mix the rosemary, garlic powder, sea salt, pepper, and lemon zest.

Situate the drumsticks in a 9-by-13-inch baking dish and sprinkle with the rosemary mixture. Bake until the chicken reaches an internal temperature of 165°F.

Nutrition (for 100g): 163 Calories 1g Fat 2g Carbohydrates 26g Protein 633mg Sodium

Chicken with Onions, Potatoes, Figs, and Carrots

Preparation Time : 5 minutes

Cooking Time : 45 minutes

Servings : 4

Difficulty Level : Average

Ingredients:

- 2 cups fingerling potatoes, halved
- 4 fresh figs, quartered
- 2 carrots, julienned
- 2 tablespoons extra-virgin olive oil
- 1 teaspoon sea salt, divided
- ¼ teaspoon freshly ground black pepper
- 4 chicken leg-thigh quarters
- 2 tablespoons chopped fresh parsley leaves

Directions:

Preheat the oven to 425°F. In a small bowl, toss the potatoes, figs, and carrots with the olive oil, ½ teaspoon of sea salt, and the pepper. Spread in a 9-by-13-inch baking dish.

Season the chicken with the rest of t sea salt. Place it on top of the vegetables. Bake until the vegetables are soft and the chicken reaches an internal temperature of 165°F. Sprinkle with the parsley and serve.

Nutrition (for 100g): 429 Calories 4g Fat 27g Carbohydrates 52g Protein 581mg Sodium

Chicken Gyros with Tzatziki

Preparation Time : 15 minutes

Cooking Time : 1 hours and 20 minutes

Servings : 6

Difficulty Level : Average

Ingredients:

- 1-pound ground chicken breast
- 1 onion, grated with excess water wrung out
- 2 tablespoons dried rosemary
- 1 tablespoon dried marjoram
- 6 garlic cloves, minced
- ½ teaspoon sea salt
- ¼ teaspoon freshly ground black pepper
- Tzatziki Sauce

Directions:

Preheat the oven to 350°F. Mix the chicken, onion, rosemary, marjoram, garlic, sea salt, and pepper using food processor. Blend until the mixture forms a paste. Alternatively, mix these ingredients in a bowl until well combined (see preparation tip).

Press the mixture into a loaf pan. Bake until it reaches 165 degrees internal temperature. Take out from the oven and let rest for 20 minutes before slicing.

Slice the gyro and spoon the tzatziki sauce over the top.

Nutrition (for 100g): 289 Calories 1g Fat 20g Carbohydrates 50g Protein 622mg Sodium

Moussaka

Preparation Time : 10 minutes

Cooking Time : 45 minutes

Servings : 8

Difficulty Level : Difficult

Ingredients:

- 5 tablespoons extra-virgin olive oil, divided
- 1 eggplant, sliced (unpeeled)
- 1 onion, chopped
- 1 green bell pepper, seeded and chopped
- 1-pound ground turkey
- 3 garlic cloves, minced
- 2 tablespoons tomato paste
- 1 (14-ounce) can chopped tomatoes, drained
- 1 tablespoon Italian seasoning
- 2 teaspoons Worcestershire sauce
- 1 teaspoon dried oregano
- ½ teaspoon ground cinnamon
- 1 cup unsweetened nonfat plain Greek yogurt
- 1 egg, beaten
- ¼ teaspoon freshly ground black pepper
- ¼ teaspoon ground nutmeg
- ¼ cup grated Parmesan cheese
- 2 tablespoons chopped fresh parsley leaves

Directions:

Preheat the oven to 400°F. Cook 3 tablespoons of olive oil until it shimmers. Add the eggplant slices and brown for 3 to 4 minutes per side. Transfer to paper towels to drain.

Return the skillet to the heat and pour the remaining 2 tablespoons of olive oil. Add the onion and green bell pepper. Continue cooking until the vegetables are soft. Remove from the pan and set aside.

Pull out the skillet to the heat and stir in the turkey. Cook for about 5 minutes, crumbling with a spoon, until browned. Stir in the garlic and cook for 30 seconds, stirring constantly.

Stir in the tomato paste, tomatoes, Italian seasoning, Worcestershire sauce, oregano, and cinnamon. Place the onion and bell pepper back to the pan. Cook for 5 minutes, stirring. Combine the yogurt, egg, pepper, nutmeg, and cheese.

Arrange half of the meat mixture in a 9-by-13-inch baking dish. Layer with half the eggplant. Add the remaining meat mixture and the remaining eggplant. Spread with the yogurt mixture. Bake until golden brown. Garnish with the parsley and serve.

Nutrition (for 100g): 338 Calories 5g Fat 16g Carbohydrates 28g Protein 569mg Sodium

Dijon and Herb Pork Tenderloin

Preparation Time : 10 minutes

Cooking Time : 30 minutes

Servings : 6

Difficulty Level : Average

Ingredients:

- ½ cup fresh Italian parsley leaves, chopped
- 3 tablespoons fresh rosemary leaves, chopped
- 3 tablespoons fresh thyme leaves, chopped
- 3 tablespoons Dijon mustard
- 1 tablespoon extra-virgin olive oil
- 4 garlic cloves, minced
- ½ teaspoon sea salt
- ¼ teaspoon freshly ground black pepper
- 1 (1½-pound) pork tenderloin

Directions:

Preheat the oven to 400°F. Blend the parsley, rosemary, thyme, mustard, olive oil, garlic, sea salt, and pepper. Process for about 30 seconds until smooth. Spread the mixture evenly over the pork and place it on a rimmed baking sheet.

Bake until the meat reaches an internal temperature of 140°F. Pull out from the oven and set aside for 10 minutes before slicing and serving.

Nutrition (for 100g): 393 Calories 3g Fat 5g Carbohydrates 74g Protein 697mg Sodium

Steak with Red Wine–Mushroom Sauce

Preparation Time : minutes plus 8 hours to marinate

Cooking Time : 20 minutes

Servings : 4

Difficulty Level : Difficult

Ingredients:

- <u>For the Marinade and Steak</u>
- 1 cup dry red wine
- 3 garlic cloves, minced
- 2 tablespoons extra-virgin olive oil
- 1 tablespoon low-sodium soy sauce
- 1 tablespoon dried thyme
- 1 teaspoon Dijon mustard
- 2 tablespoons extra-virgin olive oil
- 1 to 1½ pounds skirt steak, flat iron steak, or tri-tip steak
- <u>For the Mushroom Sauce</u>
- 2 tablespoons extra-virgin olive oil
- 1-pound cremini mushrooms, quartered
- ½ teaspoon sea salt
- 1 teaspoon dried thyme
- 1/8 teaspoon freshly ground black pepper
- 2 garlic cloves, minced
- 1 cup dry red wine

Directions:

To Make the Marinade and Steak

In a small bowl, whisk the wine, garlic, olive oil, soy sauce, thyme, and mustard. Pour into a resealable bag and add the steak. Refrigerate the steak to marinate for 4 to 8 hours. Remove the steak from the marinade and pat it dry with paper towels.

Cook the olive oil in large pan until it shimmers.

Situate the steak and cook for about 4 minutes per side until deeply browned on each side and the steak reaches an internal temperature of 140°F. Remove the steak from the skillet and put it on a plate tented with aluminum foil to keep warm, while you prepare the mushroom sauce.

When the mushroom sauce is ready, slice the steak against the grain into ½-inch-thick slices.

To Make the Mushroom Sauce

Cook oil in the same skillet over medium-high heat. Add the mushrooms, sea salt, thyme, and pepper. Cook for about 6 minutes, stirring very infrequently, until the mushrooms are browned.

Sauté the garlic. Mix in the wine, and use the side of a wooden spoon to scoop out any browned bits from the bottom of the skillet. Cook until the liquid reduces by half. Serve the mushrooms spooned over the steak.

Nutrition (for 100g): 405 Calories 5g Fat 7g Carbohydrates 33g Protein 842mg Sodium

Greek Meatballs

Preparation Time : 20 minutes

Cooking Time : 25 minutes

Servings : 4

Difficulty Level : Average

Ingredients:

- 2 whole-wheat bread slices
- 1¼ pounds ground turkey
- 1 egg
- ¼ cup seasoned whole-wheat bread crumbs
- 3 garlic cloves, minced
- ¼ red onion, grated
- ¼ cup chopped fresh Italian parsley leaves
- 2 tablespoons chopped fresh mint leaves
- 2 tablespoons chopped fresh oregano leaves
- ½ teaspoon sea salt
- ¼ teaspoon freshly ground black pepper

Directions:

Preheat the oven to 350°F. Situate parchment paper or aluminum foil onto the baking sheet. Run the bread under water to wet it, and squeeze out any excess. Shred wet bread into small pieces and place it in a medium bowl.

Add the turkey, egg, bread crumbs, garlic, red onion, parsley, mint, oregano, sea salt, and pepper. Mix well. Form the mixture into ¼-cup-size balls. Place the meatballs on the prepared sheet and bake for about 25 minutes, or until the internal temperature reaches 165°F.

Nutrition (for 100g): 350 Calories 6g Fat 10g Carbohydrates 42g Protein 842mg Sodium

Lamb with String Beans

Preparation Time : 10 minutes

Cooking Time : 1 hour

Servings : 6

Difficulty Level : Difficult

Ingredients:

- ¼ cup extra-virgin olive oil, divided
- 6 lamb chops, trimmed of extra fat
- 1 teaspoon sea salt, divided
- ½ teaspoon freshly ground black pepper
- 2 tablespoons tomato paste
- 1½ cups hot water
- 1-pound green beans, trimmed and halved crosswise
- 1 onion, chopped
- 2 tomatoes, chopped

Directions:

Cook 2 tablespoons of olive oil in large skillet until it shimmers. Season the lamb chops with ½ teaspoon of sea salt and 1/8 teaspoon of pepper. Cook the lamb in the hot oil for about 4 minutes per side until browned on both sides. Situate the meat to a platter and set aside.

Position the skillet back to the heat and put the remaining 2 tablespoons of olive oil. Heat until it shimmers.

In a bowl, melt the tomato paste in the hot water. Add it to the hot skillet along with the green beans, onion, tomatoes, and the remaining ½ teaspoon of sea salt and ¼ teaspoon of pepper. Bring to a simmer, using a spoon's side to scrape browned bits from the bottom of the pan.

Return the lamb chops to the pan. Allow to boil and adjust the heat to medium-low. Simmer for 45 minutes until the beans are soft, adding additional water as needed to adjust the sauce's thickness.

Nutrition (for 100g): 439 Calories 4g Fat 10g Carbohydrates 50g Protein 745mg Sodium

Chicken in Tomato-Balsamic Pan Sauce

Preparation Time : 10 minutes

Cooking Time : 20 minutes

Servings : 4

Difficulty Level : Average

Ingredients

- 2 (8 oz. or 226.7 g each) boneless chicken breasts, skinless
- ½ tsp. salt
- ½ tsp. ground pepper
- 3 tbsps. extra-virgin olive oil
- ½ c. halved cherry tomatoes
- 2 tbsps. sliced shallot
- ¼ c. balsamic vinegar
- 1 tbsp. minced garlic
- 1 tbsp. toasted fennel seeds, crushed
- 1 tbsp. butter

Directions:

Slice the chicken breasts into 4 pieces and beat them with a mallet till it reaches a thickness of a ¼ inch. Use ¼ teaspoons of pepper and salt to coat the chicken. Heat two tablespoons of oil in a skillet and keep the heat to a medium. Cook the chicken breasts on both sides for three minutes. Place it to a serving plate and cover it with foil to keep it warm.

Add one tablespoon oil, shallot, and tomatoes in a pan and cook till it softens. Add vinegar and boil the mix till the vinegar gets reduced by half. Put fennel seeds, garlic, salt, and pepper and cook for about four minutes. Pull it out from the heat and stir it with butter. Pour this sauce over chicken and serve.

Nutrition (for 100g): 294 Calories 17g Fat 10g Carbohydrates 2g Protein 639mg Sodium

Brown Rice, Feta, Fresh Pea, and Mint Salad

Preparation Time : 10 minutes

Cooking Time : 25 minutes

Servings : 4

Difficulty Level : Easy

Ingredients:

- 2 c. brown rice
- 3 c. water
- Salt
- 5 oz. or 141.7 g crumbled feta cheese
- 2 c. cooked peas
- ½ c. chopped mint, fresh
- 2 tbsps. olive oil
- Salt and pepper

Directions:

Place the brown rice, water, and salt into a saucepan over medium heat, cover, and bring to boiling point. Turn the lower heat and allow it to cook until the water has dissolved and the rice is soft but chewy. Leave to cool completely

Add the feta, peas, mint, olive oil, salt, and pepper to a salad bowl with the cooled rice and toss to combine Serve and enjoy!

Nutrition (for 100g): 613 Calories 18.2g Fat 45g Carbohydrates 12g Protein 755mg Sodium

Whole Grain Pita Bread Stuffed with Olives and Chickpeas

Preparation Time : 10 minutes

Cooking Time : 20 minutes

Servings : 2

Difficulty Level : Average

Ingredients:

- 2 wholegrain pita pockets
- 2 tbsps. olive oil
- 2 garlic cloves, chopped
- 1 onion, chopped
- ½ tsp. cumin
- 10 black olives, chopped
- 2 c. cooked chickpeas
- Salt and pepper

Directions:

Slice open the pita pockets and set aside Adjust your heat to medium and set a pan in place. Add in the olive oil and heat. Mix in the garlic, onion, and cumin to the hot pan and stir as the onions soften and the cumin is fragrant Add the olives, chickpeas, salt, and pepper and toss everything together until the chickpeas become golden

Set the pan from heat and use your wooden spoon to roughly mash the chickpeas so that some are intact and some are crushed Heat your pita pockets in the microwave, in the oven, or on a clean pan on the stove

Fill them with your chickpea mixture and enjoy!

Nutrition (for 100g): 503 Calories 19g Fat 14g Carbohydrates 15.7g Protein 798mg Sodium

Roasted Carrots with Walnuts and Cannellini Beans

Preparation Time : 10 minutes

Cooking Time : 45 minutes

Servings : 4

Difficulty Level : Average

Ingredients:

- 4 peeled carrots, chopped
- 1 c. walnuts
- 1 tbsp. honey
- 2 tbsps. olive oil
- 2 c. canned cannellini beans, drained
- 1 fresh thyme sprig
- Salt and pepper

Directions:

Set oven to 400 F/204 C and line a baking tray or roasting pan with baking paper Lay the carrots and walnuts onto the lined tray or pan Sprinkle olive oil and honey over the carrots and walnuts and give everything a rub to make sure each piece is coated Scatter the beans onto the tray and nestle into the carrots and walnuts

Add the thyme and sprinkle everything with salt and pepper Set tray in your oven and roast for about 40 minutes.

Serve and enjoy

Nutrition (for 100g): 385 Calories 27g Fat 6g Carbohydrates 18g Protein 859mg Sodium

Seasoned Buttered Chicken

Preparation Time : 10 minutes

Cooking Time : 25 minutes

Servings : 4

Difficulty Level : Average

Ingredients:

- ½ c. Heavy Whipping Cream
- 1 tbsp. Salt
- ½ c. Bone Broth
- 1 tbsp. Pepper
- 4 tbsps. Butter
- 4 Chicken Breast Halves

Directions:

Place cooking pan on your oven over medium heat and add in one tablespoon of butter. Once the butter is warm and melted, place the chicken in and cook for five minutes on either side. At the end of this time, the chicken should be cooked through and golden; if it is, go ahead and place it on a plate.

Next, you are going to add the bone broth into the warm pan. Add heavy whipping cream, salt, and pepper. Then, leave the pan alone until your sauce begins to simmer. Allow this process to happen for five minutes to let the sauce thicken up.

Finally, you are going to add the rest of your butter and the chicken back into the pan. Be sure to use a spoon to place the sauce over your chicken and smother it completely. Serve

Nutrition (for 100g): 350 Calories 25g Fat 10g Carbohydrates 25g Protein 869mg Sodium

Double Cheesy Bacon Chicken

Preparation Time : 10 minutes

Cooking Time : 30 minutes

Servings : 4

Difficulty Level : Easy

Ingredients:

- 4 oz. or 113 g. Cream Cheese
- 1 c. Cheddar Cheese
- 8 strips Bacon
- Sea salt
- Pepper
- 2 Garlic cloves, finely chopped
- Chicken Breast
- 1 tbsp. Bacon Grease or Butter

Directions:

Ready the oven to 400 F/204 C Slice the chicken breasts in half to make them thin

Season with salt, pepper, and garlic Grease a baking pan with butter and place chicken breasts into it. Add the cream cheese and cheddar cheese on top of the breasts

Add bacon slices as well Place the pan to the oven for 30 minutes Serve hot

Nutrition (for 100g): 610 Calories 32g Fat 3g Carbohydrates 38g Protein 759mg Sodium

Shrimps with Lemon and Pepper

Preparation Time : 10 minutes

Cooking Time : 10 minutes

Servings : 4

Difficulty Level : Easy

Ingredients:

- 40 deveined shrimps, peeled
- 6 minced garlic cloves
- Salt and black pepper
- 3 tbsps. olive oil
- ¼ tsp. sweet paprika
- A pinch crushed red pepper flake
- ¼ tsp. grated lemon zest
- 3 tbsps. Sherry or another wine
- 1½ tbsps. sliced chives
- Juice of 1 lemon

Directions:

Adjust your heat to medium-high and set a pan in place.

Add oil and shrimp, sprinkle with pepper and salt and cook for 1 minute Add paprika, garlic and pepper flakes, stir and cook for 1 minute. Gently stir in sherry and allow to cook for an extra minute

Take shrimp off the heat, add chives and lemon zest, stir and transfer shrimp to plates. Add lemon juice all over and serve

Nutrition (for 100g): 140 Calories 1g Fat 5g Carbohydrates 18g Protein 694mg Sodium

Breaded and Spiced Halibut

Preparation Time : 5 minutes

Cooking Time : 25 minutes

Servings : 4

Difficulty Level : Easy

Ingredients:

- ¼ c. chopped fresh chives
- ¼ c. chopped fresh dill
- ¼ tsp. ground black pepper
- ¾ c. panko breadcrumbs
- 1 tbsp. extra-virgin olive oil
- 1 tsp. finely grated lemon zest
- 1 tsp. sea salt
- 1/3 c. chopped fresh parsley
- 4 (6 oz. or 170 g. each) halibut fillets

Directions:

In a medium bowl, mix olive oil and the rest ingredients except halibut fillets and breadcrumbs

Place halibut fillets into the mixture and marinate for 30 minutes Preheat your oven to 400 F/204 C Set a foil to a baking sheet, grease with cooking spray Dip the fillets to the breadcrumbs and put to the baking sheet Cook in the oven for 20 minutes Serve hot

Nutrition (for 100g): 667 Calories 24.5g Fat 2g Carbohydrates 54.8g Protein 756mg Sodium

Curry Salmon with Mustard

Preparation Time : 10 minutes

Cooking Time : 20 minutes

Servings : 4

Difficulty Level : Easy

Ingredients:

- ¼ tsp. ground red pepper or chili powder
- ¼ tsp. turmeric, ground
- ¼ tsp. salt
- 1 tsp. honey
- ¼ tsp. garlic powder
- 2 tsps. whole grain mustard
- 4 (6 oz. or 170 g. each) salmon fillets

Directions:

In a bowl mix mustard and the rest ingredients except salmon Preheat the oven to 350 F/176 C Grease a baking dish with cooking spray. Place salmon on baking dish with skin side down and spread evenly mustard mixture on top of fillets Place into the oven and cook for 10-15 minutes or until flaky

Nutrition (for 100g): 324 Calories 18.9g Fat 1.3g Carbohydrates 34g Protein 593mg Sodium

Walnut-Rosemary Crusted Salmon

Preparation Time : 10 minutes

Cooking Time : 25 minutes

Servings : 4

Difficulty Level : Average

Ingredients:

- 1 lb. or 450 g. frozen skinless salmon fillet
- 2 tsps. Dijon mustard
- 1 clove garlic, minced
- ¼ tsp. lemon zest
- ½ tsp. honey
- ½ tsp. kosher salt
- 1 tsp. freshly chopped rosemary
- 3 tbsps. panko breadcrumbs
- ¼ tsp. crushed red pepper
- 3 tbsps. chopped walnuts
- 2 tsp. extra-virgin olive oil

Directions:

Prepare the oven to 420 F/215 C and use parchment paper to line a rimmed baking sheet. In a bowl combine mustard, lemon zest, garlic, lemon juice, honey, rosemary, crushed red pepper, and salt. In another bowl mix walnut, panko, and 1 tsp oil Place parchments paper on the baking sheet and lay the salmon on it

Spread mustard mixture on the fish, and top with the panko mixture. Spray the rest of olive oil lightly on the salmon. Bake for about 10 -12 minutes or until the salmon is being separated by a fork Serve hot

Nutrition (for 100g): 222 Calories 12g Fat 4g Carbohydrates 0.8g Protein 812mg Sodium

Quick Tomato Spaghetti

Preparation Time : 10 minutes

Cooking Time : 25 minutes

Servings : 4

Difficulty Level : Average

Ingredients:

- 8 oz. or 226.7g spaghetti
- 3 tbsps. olive oil
- 4 garlic cloves, sliced
- 1 jalapeno, sliced
- 2 c. cherry tomatoes
- Salt and pepper
- 1 tsp. balsamic vinegar
- ½ c. Parmesan, grated

Directions:

Boil a large pot of water on medium flame. Add a pinch of salt and bring to a boil then add the spaghetti. Allow cooking for 8 minutes. While the pasta cooks, heat the oil in a skillet and add the garlic and jalapeno. Cook for an extra 1 minute then stir in the tomatoes, pepper, and salt.

Cook for 5-7 minutes until the tomatoes' skins burst.

Add the vinegar and remove off heat. Drain spaghetti well and mix it with the tomato sauce. Sprinkle with cheese and serve right away.

Nutrition (for 100g): 298 Calories 13.5g Fat 10.5g Carbohydrates 8g Protein 749mg Sodium

Chili Oregano Baked Cheese

Preparation Time : 10 minutes

Cooking Time : 25 minutes

Servings : 4

Difficulty Level : Easy

Ingredients:

- 8 oz. or 226.7g feta cheese
- 4 oz. or 113g mozzarella, crumbled
- 1 sliced chili pepper
- 1 tsp. dried oregano
- 2 tbsps. olive oil

Directions:

Place the feta cheese in a small deep-dish baking pan. Top with the mozzarella then season with pepper slices and oregano. cover your pan with lid. Bake in the preheated oven at 350 F/176 C for 20 minutes. Serve the cheese and enjoy it.

Nutrition (for 100g): 292 Calories 24.2g Fat 5.7g Carbohydrates 2g Protein 733mg Sodium

311. Crispy Italian Chicken

Preparation Time : 10 minutes

Cooking Time : 30 minutes

Servings : 4

Difficulty Level : Easy

Ingredients:

- 4 chicken legs
- 1 tsp. dried basil
- 1 tsp. dried oregano
- Salt and pepper
- 3 tbsps. olive oil
- 1 tbsp. balsamic vinegar

Directions:

Season the chicken well with basil, and oregano. Using a skillet, add oil and heat. Add the chicken in the hot oil. Let each side cook for 5 minutes until golden then cover the skillet with a lid.

Adjust your heat to medium and cook for 10 minutes on one side then flip the chicken repeatedly, cooking for another 10 minutes until crispy. Serve the chicken and enjoy.

Nutrition (for 100g): 262 Calories 13.9g Fat 11g Carbohydrates 32.6g Protein 693mg Sodium